Off The Couch Into the
War for Hearts and Minds

Sue and Chris

Everything achieved was made possible by caring and compassionate people like you.

you, in fact, are responsible for an entire school for girls. Hearts and minds are won one at a time and the progress is never over. Thank you for your support over the years.

Bill

Off The Couch Into the War for Hearts and Minds

❖ ❖ ❖

Budd E. Mackenzie

ISBN: 1517720060
ISBN 13: 9781517720063
Library of Congress Control Number: 2015916768
CreateSpace Independent Publishing Platform
North Charleston, South Carolina

Acknowledgments

❖ ❖ ❖

Were it not for the thousands of people who have come forward over the years to assist Trust in Education by donating their time and money, there would be no book and I would not have discovered how rewarding humanitarian aid work can be. Givers are happier and consequently more enjoyable to be around. I'm grateful to have had their support and company.

I'm also inspired by the courageous women in Afghanistan who must "lean forward" in multiple aspects of their lives to secure the most basic freedoms. They and the Afghan men who support them are on the front line often putting their lives at risk. They serve as a daily reminder of how fortunate I am.

Nabi Tawakali's knowledge, connections, cultural sensitivity, humor, unwavering support and guidance defy description. Much of what Trust in Education accomplishes is thanks to Nabi. He is the friend who is always there.

Khaled Hosseini's work, deeds, support, and advice have been invaluable over the nine years I've known him. Better than anyone, he's able to communicate how critical it is that we not standby and tolerate intolerable conditions.

As for the book itself there have been several friends who read and improved drafts. My cousin, Ralph Comstock, spent countless hours during two summer vacations in Montana, focused on every word, sentence, paragraph and chapter. We had many lengthy discussions about what to write and how. He's a wordsmith. Tammy Miller's triple berry pie and huckleberry ice cream provided the energy boost he needed when he began to fade.

Lynn Deckert was amused by how I sprinkle commas at will without regard to punctuation protocol. I throw them in whenever I think there should be a pause. Her favorite topic in the book is also mine—gender equality or rather the lack thereof.

Jil Plummer, author of *Remember to Remember*, *Amber Dust*, and *Caravan to Armageddon*, devoted hours discussing, improving and clarifying passages with me. I'm envious of her writing skills and insights. Jack Howell was the first to say "there aren't enough stories," and he was right. That took a year to correct.

Patty Spinks devoted hours to improving the photographs always willing to help on a moments notice

Victoria Wang, Trust in Education's Project Director, relentlessly poured over multiple drafts, including the final, in an effort "to make it perfect." Let me know if we succeeded, although, bear in mind I prefer positive reinforcement.

The book has passed through multiple filters, each of which invaluably improved its focus. Trust in Education is the sum of many parts. So it is only fitting that the book is, as well.

Contents page

Prologue

❖ ❖ ❖

ON SUNDAY MORNING APRIL 6, 2003, I had two choices—go to the health club and exercise or lie on the couch and read the paper. Had I chosen to exercise that day, there would be no book and I'd be thinner. That's not entirely true; I would not be thinner. Include me among the millions of Americans who will do everything to remain healthy except eat right and exercise!

When reading the Sunday paper my first chore is to toss onto the floor the ads and sections of the paper which are of no interest to me, which usually includes the Parade magazine. However, that Sunday, I read a Parade article, got off the couch and made a call that proved to be life altering. For the last thirteen years I have been engaged in the "war on poverty" in Afghanistan. Out of necessity, I was unwillingly thrust into the war for hearts and minds both there and here.

There are times when I think the hearts and minds war cannot be won, particularly when listening to the vitriolic rhetoric embraced by a man who aspires to be President. Perhaps it can't be won. But, it also needn't be lost. It will only be lost if we let it, a compelling reason to enlist others to get off the couch.

I've written this book for several reasons. First, I strongly urge everyone to join in the struggle against poverty and for hearts and minds. Second, there are things I have experienced, learned and observed that will be as astounding to others as they were to me. Third, this can also serve as a primer for burgeoning social entrepreneurs. They will benefit from what I have learned and the mistakes I have made.

Finally, and most importantly, after more than twenty trips to Kabul over ten years, I, like everyone I've met who has spent time in Afghanistan, have developed an affinity for its people. Afghans are well known for their hospitality and generosity. Guests are honored, respected and to be protected. Were we in their shoes and they in ours, they would come to our aid. Given our involvement in the region over the past 36 years, we should welcome the opportunity to do the same.

Of course, I would also like readers to conclude, as thousands have, that Trust in Education has proven itself worthy of their support.

CHAPTER 1

The Journey Begins

❖ ❖ ❖

ON MARCH 22, 2003, THE Lafayette City Council held a public meeting to discuss whether it should send a letter to Washington either supporting or opposing the invasion of Iraq. The letter itself was of no real consequence; the United States had invaded Iraq two days earlier. Nonetheless, a hundred or so concerned citizens came to argue the merits of the invasion.

I listened long enough to know I did not need to stay long. Most were opposed to the invasion—been there, heard that. I'd heard all the arguments before on the "Beserkely" campus in the late sixties, when we were engaged in the controversial Vietnam "conflict" (later acknowledged as a war). The only difference was, in the sixties, I wore flowered shirts, bell-bottom trousers, a beaded macramé belt, and a pukka-shell necklace partially sheltered by shoulder-length hair.

In the late sixties and early seventies campus debates evolved into student rallies, street marches by the thousands, blockades, violent confrontations with the police, and riots. The National Guard, bearing rifles with fixed bayonets and gas masks, was called to the Berkeley campus several times, often for days. Tear gas permeated the air for weeks during and after the National Guard's visits. Bank of America's branch on Telegraph Avenue had its glass panes shattered so often, they finally replaced the windows with brick. The windows still have not returned. "On strike, shut it down," "Hell no, we won't go," "All we are saying is, 'Give peace a chance'", and "We won't fight another rich man's war" were slogans of the day. The fraternity favorite, of course, was "Burn the bra," which over time fell victim to the force of gravity.

The Vietnam War tore our country apart. Tens of thousands enlisted or were drafted and served. Thousands who refused to serve were prosecuted. Judgments were made as to who was and wasn't a "conscientious objector". Those who failed the conscientious-objector test faced extensive jail time. Some fled to Canada.

Demonstrators were beaten, arrested, and imprisoned. At the Kent State University campus four student demonstrators were killed, and nine others were wounded. Ideological lines tested relationships among families and friends. Heated hallway debates were held in dorms late into the night questioning whether we should volunteer and whether draftees should have the right to refuse military service without facing punishment. If draftees could refuse service with impunity, was an all-volunteer army possible? Many argued that an all-volunteer army wasn't desirable.

Initially students received educational deferments from being in the draft pool. These deferments were subsequently eliminated, and a lottery draft system was instituted. I sat next to a radio with friends for well over two anxious hours until my number was called. Friends with low numbers knew they were likely to be drafted. Mine was in the 120s—not high enough to be considered "safe." The Coast and National Guards received thousands of applications as did the Peace Corps. These were preferable alternatives that made it possible to avoid military service. The escape routes filled up quickly, and the rumor was you needed to know someone to get in.

A classmate came to class one day wearing braces having learned they were a draft disqualifier, at least temporarily. Prior to his physical, another classmate drank gallons of Gatorade, a popular sweet energy boost drink for athletes. He'd heard it would raise his blood pressure beyond what was acceptable. His urine was the "clearest" they had ever seen at the draft center. As I recall, the Gatorade induced high blood pressure strategy didn't work but he wasn't drafted. No one I knew was drafted.

I believe the absence of a draft extended the wars in Afghanistan and Iraq far beyond what the public would have tolerated had their sons and daughters been forced to go. My father, an Air Force colonel and World War II veteran, held steadfast to the principle that "right or wrong, it's your country." No one had the right to deny service when called, without paying a price.

During vacations I visited my father in Pocatello, Idaho, where I was a "bleeding-heart liberal." On the Berkeley campus "flaming, radical, pinko, communist peaceniks" accused me of being a "fascist-pig reactionary." How others assess our political identity, like real estate, depends on three factors—location, location, and location.

While listening to the debate in Lafayette, I became concerned that history was about to repeat itself. As of that weekend, we were engaged in two wars: one in Afghanistan and the other in Iraq. They would certainly become unpopular and divisive. Hadn't we learned anything from Vietnam? I began searching for something constructive we could do to help the effort in Afghanistan that both sides of the debate could comfortably embrace.

Fifteen days later on April 6, 2003, while lying on the couch, the answer literally fell out of the Sunday newspaper while I was disposing of advertising inserts. Greg Mortensen's photo appeared on the cover of *Parade* magazine along with the caption "fighting terror with books." After reading about his work building schools in Pakistan and Afghanistan, I decided to contact him.

It took six weeks to reach him by phone; understandable, given the circulation of *Parade* magazine was over 30 million. After an hour of due diligence questioning, including asking how much he was being paid by his nonprofit corporation, Central Asia Institute, I asked what it would cost to build another school in Afghanistan. He replied, "twenty-five thousand dollars." That proved to be less than half the final cost, but it sounded like a manageable number.

I told Greg to pick another village for a school, and said my friends and I would raise what he felt was needed. He had four locations in the pipeline at the time, so I asked him to select one we could fund. He chose the village of Lalander, Afghanistan, and agreed to speak at Acalanes, a local high school that my children had had the good fortune of attending.

Everyone has a few dependable friends who can be counted on to volunteer when called. I called mine, and my first campaign to raise money to build a school in Afghanistan began. The wheels began to turn and the train slowly left the station. The question at the outset was whether enough passengers would get on board. Note to organizers: start the train moving. Don't wait for a critical mass of support to build. If you wait, the first few aboard will debate *ad nauseam* the merits of leaving and what to do next. Remain the conductor until you're replaceable.

Raising twenty-five thousand dollars in Lafayette to build a school in Afghanistan sounded easy. Lafayette is an affluent community that spent over one million dollars on repairing and building Little League baseball fields. I had no idea how much resistance we would encounter to what for me seemed uncontroversial.

Early in the campaign, members of a Girl Scout troop decided to raise funds to build the school and, filled with enthusiasm, they set up a table in front of a local grocery store. Shortly thereafter, I received a troubling call from someone working with the Girl Scouts who was concerned that the organization would be identified with the project. She advised me that the fact the girls were Girl Scouts should not be mentioned in any news articles or fundraising materials. Also, she added, they were not to wear their uniforms while soliciting money. This was my first encounter with the phenomenon of "protecting the label."

I had not sought or intended to seek the endorsement of the Girl Scouts organization; neither had I intended to publicize that the girls were scouts.

They had simply chosen to become involved and, like most children, were also members of other groups. It seemed odd that the Girl Scout organization did not want recognition for what their members had decided to do on their own. Nonetheless, I had been duly warned. I still buy their cookies—I can't say "no" to Caramel deLites, nor their messengers.

The suggestion was made that I seek approval for the project from Lafayette's city council. Presumably, this would help legitimize the effort. At the suggestion of Lafayette's city manager, I prepared a proclamation for the council to consider. At the first hearing no action was taken, and the matter was continued for several weeks.

It became obvious that approval by the city council would not be a slam-dunk. The proclamation became political. Well in advance of the first city-council hearing, I knew their approval wasn't necessary to achieve our goal. We were well on our way to raising the full amount I was told we would need to build the school.

A week before the second hearing I decided to not pursue approval of the proclamation and advised the city clerk that it should be dropped from the calendar. I subsequently received a call from Carl Anduri, a council member, asking me why it had been dropped. I explained that I didn't want our project to become controversial or political.

Carl informed me that his wife, Sharon, and others had planned to attend the hearing and support the proclamation. Following our conversation, I called the clerk and asked to put the matter back on the calendar. I wanted to learn why issuing a proclamation supporting the construction of a school in Afghanistan was becoming controversial. Moreover, if Sharon and her friends were willing to support the request, so should I.

During the second hearing, one council member asked whether I was requesting money or city staff time. I wasn't. Another commented that he was concerned about voting on matters beyond the city limits. I explained that a considerable and growing number of Lafayette residents had decided it was a good idea and that I had assumed the council would want to lend its support. Why *not* support building a school in Afghanistan given the history of U.S. involvement there?

I also thought that support by Lafayette's city council would be well received by the village leaders in Lalander. The goal from the beginning had been to link our village with theirs. Therefore, it made sense to establish a connection between our leaders and theirs.

After very little discussion, the council voted four to one in favor of the proclamation. The "no" vote was cast by a council member concerned about cultural imperialism. I didn't understand his argument then and I still don't now. How can funding the construction of a school be culturally imperialistic when everything taught there would be by Afghan teachers employed by Afghanistan's Ministry of Education? The village had asked for help, and our support was unconditional. I am very grateful for Carl's call and Sharon's support. Without it, I would have taken the easy way out and dropped it from the council's calendar.

Thus my journey began while lying on my couch with a *Parade* magazine falling to the floor. Had Greg Mortenson's photo been inside the magazine and not on the cover, I would be kayaking on the Swan River in Montana right now instead of writing this chapter. I had never opened a *Parade* magazine before and haven't since.

Was my reading the *Parade* article a coincidence? I've had too many intervening events after this life-altering magazine cover to attribute them all to coincidence. Shakespeare may have been right when he wrote, "the world is a stage and all the men and women merely players." [1] I may well be "merely a player" on the world's stage with the script being revealed to me no more than one page at a time.

CHAPTER 2

Here is Not a Place

❖   ❖   ❖

QUESTION AND ANSWER SESSIONS AFTER presentations can be controversial. At the end of one a man stood at the back of the room and shouted, "How much money have you donated to the San Ramon school district?" As hostile as his question was, he was being honest. He dared say publicly what many won't say to me privately. Why help Afghanistan when we have problems here?

One response I could have given was, "Why would I contribute to San Ramon schools? I live in Lafayette. In fact, why should I care about educating any children? Mine have graduated from college and moved away". The answer I should have given then and would give now is, "Here is not a place. Here is where you define it to be".

Before 2005, my "here" didn't extend beyond Lafayette. I contributed to and volunteered for organizations that benefited my children, my neighbors, family, and friends. In 2005 when I first visited Afghanistan, I came face-to-face with abject poverty in what was then the fifth-poorest country in the world.

Thousands of men linger on the streets of Kabul with nothing to do. What few women there are walk quickly, staring straight ahead, so as not to be noticed or accosted. Babies lay cradled in their mothers' arms, both dependent upon spare change and the generosity of others to survive. Pickup trucks loaded with armed men, some with mounted guns, speed by never giving way to people, cars, or donkey carts in their paths. Hundreds of men, women, and children, some missing limbs, plead at car windows for money. Police in insufficient numbers, carrying automatic weapons, are positioned where terrorists are most likely to strike, knowing that no one is safe anywhere or anytime.

I knew by the end of my 2005 trip to Kabul that I could not resume the sheltered life I had led before. I had experienced firsthand the deplorable conditions in Afghanistan and by then knew that they were in large measure consequences of our involvement there. The sights, sounds, and smells of poverty are life altering and unforgettable.

The man who had shouted during my talk argued with me afterward. His "here" didn't expand, and mine didn't contract by the conclusion of our conversation. What everyone does, consciously and unconsciously, is divide the world into "here" and "there" and "them" and "us." Therein lies the greatest challenge of our time—convincing others to adopt a broader and more inclusive view of the world. No one should ever need to defend his or her decision to help anyone anywhere in the world.

CHAPTER 3

Afghanistan—Why Care?

❖ ❖ ❖

THE SOVIET INVASION OF AFGHANISTAN in 1979 marked the beginning of the
United States' first significant commitment there. That's what I wrote
and thought for years until I stumbled upon an interview of Zbigniew
Brzezinski, national security advisor to President Carter at that time. In
the interview, Brzezinski acknowledged that until former CIA Director
Robert Gates revealed otherwise in 1998, the official version of history was that CIA aid to the mujahedeen in Pakistan began in 1980, after
the Soviet Army invaded Afghanistan on December 24, 1979. The truth
is that American intelligence services began to aid the mujahideen six
months before the Soviet intervention:

"The reality, secretly guarded until now, is completely otherwise,"
Brzezinski said. "Indeed, it was July 3, 1979 that President Carter
signed the first directive for secret aid to the opponents of the pro-
Soviet regime in Kabul. That very day, I wrote a note to the President
strongly stating my opinion that this aid was going to induce a Soviet
military intervention."

Brzezinski was asked whether he regretted the decision. He responded: "Regret what? That secret operation was an excellent idea.
It had the effect of drawing the Russians into the Afghan trap and you
want me to regret it?" The day the Soviets officially crossed the border, I again wrote to President Carter, "We now have the opportunity

of giving to the USSR its Vietnam war." Indeed, for almost ten years Moscow had to carry on a war unsupportable by the government—a conflict which brought about the demoralization and finally the breakup of the Soviet empire.

What is most important to the history of the world? The Taliban or the collapse of the Soviet empire? Some stirred up Muslims or the liberation of Central Europe and the end of the cold war?" [2]

It should be noted that there are at least two editions of the magazine; with perhaps the sole exception of the Library of Congress the version sent to the United States is shorter than that of the French. The Brzezinski interview was not included in the edition distributed in the United States. It's not known or at least not reported whether the magazine removed the interview at someone's request.

The "stirred up Muslims" were responsible for September 11, 2001, and this group now includes the Taliban, Al-Qaeda, and ISIS. Afghanistan has suffered the consequences of over thirty-seven years of war. Support of the "stirred up Muslims" may have been worth it to Central Europe, but the same cannot be said for the United States or Afghanistan.

Anyone interested in the history of the United States involvement in Afghanistan should read *Charlie Wilson's War* by George Crile. The book chronicles what the author describes as the Central Intelligence Agency's largest, most expensive and successful clandestine operation in history. The objectives of the operation were simple: Supply training and weapons to the mujahideen (freedom fighters) in support of their *jihad* (holy war) against the Soviet "infidels" and thereby "turn Afghanistan into the Soviet Union's Vietnam".

Along with other nations, the United States supplied billions of dollars in weapons to the warlords and mujahideen through Pakistan. Afghanistan became a cold war "checkerboard" upon which men chosen and trained in Pakistan waged war against the Soviets. By the time the

Soviets were driven out of Afghanistan in January, 1989, the mujahideen were well trained, seasoned fighters, armed to the hilt with modern weaponry and beholden to no external control. As many as thirty thousand "holy warriors" traveled from other countries to join in the war against the Soviets.

Nine months after the Soviet Union was driven out of Kabul, the Berlin Wall fell and by December 1991, the Soviet Union ceased to exist. While historians may disagree on the extent, all recognize the impact the war in Afghanistan had on the outcome of the Cold War and Central Europe. The cost to Afghanistan included 1.5 million lives. Five million Afghans fled their homes and became refugees in a world whose ability and tolerance to absorb refugees was already strained. The United States washed its hands of any responsibility in Afghanistan as of 1993 when all humanitarian aid was withdrawn. There were no roads, no schools, just a destroyed country. Warlords, Islamic extremists, drug lords, and defenseless Afghans fought over what scant resources remained.

On October 21, 2001, following the tragic events of September 11, the United States invaded Afghanistan to search for Osama bin Laden and Al-Qaeda. Osama bin Laden was ultimately killed on May 2, 2011, almost ten years later. The "get Bin Laden mission" accomplished, our reason for invading Afghanistan no longer justified staying, but we had already assumed the role of "nation builders" which we continue performing today.

Afghanistan is sadly ranked among the poorest countries in the world with an annual per capita income, last reported in 2014, of $413.43— three percent of the world's average. Of the thirty-seven years of war fought inside Afghanistan, the United States either financed or waged twenty-eight. If there is one thing every visitor learns about Afghanistan, it's that over ninety-nine percent of its people don't want to fight or kill anyone. They want what these girls want.

We must not abandon the Afghan people as we did in 1993. History has favored Americans with an opportunity to join with Afghans in remedying the unintended yet foreseeable consequences of "Charlie Wilson's War." We cannot reverse history, but we certainly can embrace the role we have been invited to play and, under the circumstances, the least we should do is try.

YEAR BY YEAR

It has now been thirteen years since this life and mind-altering experience began in 2003. It's one I never intended to take beyond raising funds to build one school. In 2005 I began writing and sending newsletters to supporters and people interested in Afghanistan. There are now over two thousand names on the mailing list. The newsletters enable me to share challenges, successes, setbacks, experiences, observations, mistakes and failures.

I went back through the newsletters. Reviewing them has been a trip down memory lane. I've recalled more than I originally reported, but don't hold me responsible for timing or historical accuracy given the decline in my random access memory. Whenever a new fact goes into memory, two fall out—a decline many baby boomers share. I've included stories, personal experiences and observations in what follows and, to the extent possible, placed them in chronological order.

CHAPTER 4

Events in 2005

❖ ❖ ❖

IN OCTOBER, 2014, KHALED NEMATI came to my Lafayette office to volunteer. During our conversation I mentioned that the school would be built in Lalander. A broad smile broke out on his face as he said, "I'm from Lalander. My family is from Lalander." Khaled and his family live only a few miles from my office. From that moment on I knew I would have "insiders", people who would be direct links between the village and me.

Khaled's father, Raymond, visited Lalander the following month and phoned back with some troubling news. The project manager hired by Central Asia Institute to build the school was building a house for his family with the same men and materials he was using to build the school. The men were working on the project manager's home, and it didn't appear the school would be ready when it was due to open in March, 2015. I forwarded this information to Greg Mortensen and didn't receive a reply. It was now a year and a half after we had begun our fundraising effort and Greg Mortensen had failed to provide any progress reports. Notwithstanding family and friends who urged me to stay home, I decided to travel to Afghanistan to see the situation myself.

I had an obligation to the hundreds of people who had raised and contributed over thirty thousand dollars to the project to verify that their time and money was being well spent. I had read *Charlie's Wilson's War* and wanted first-hand knowledge of how our involvement in Afghanistan had impacted the country. I must also admit there was an element of adventure that was enticing. Out of the proverbial box is not where I want to live, but it's where life's most interesting moments seem to occur.

It rained our first day in Kabul. Rainy days are considered "beautiful" because there is less dust in the air. Most of the streets are dirt and very dry. It took six weeks for our lungs to dislodge and discharge the dust we consumed while in Kabul.

The paved roads have potholes so deep they flatten tires, destroy suspension systems, and catapult passengers into the roof of their vehicles. Speeding cars, swerving to avoid these hazards, come face to face in showdowns that are not quickly resolved.

To their credit, however, angry motorists don't lean on their horns, but rely mainly on hand gestures to express their rage.

The downtown traffic in Kabul is like none I've ever experienced. Cars attack the streets like ants whose hill has just been kicked. No one feels bound by lanes and no one gives way easily to vehicles or people trying to cross the street. Policemen controlling traffic are ignored. Everyone drives as fast as possible and faster than is safe.

The cars, like ants, come head to head but seldom run into each other. I only saw one traffic accident. A young girl was struck by a speeding car. Her motionless body was lifted into the back seat of the car that hit her and raced away to the nearest hospital. Within minutes, traffic and life on the street resumed to what Afghans perceive as normal.

DOWNTOWN KABUL

Raymond and I stayed in the Mustafa hotel in downtown Kabul. It had been a favored hangout for journalists and adventurers during the Taliban reign. The Mustafa hotel is located one block from "Chicken Street," a street lined with shops on both sides, some no larger than a linen closet. Once a tourist favorite, it's now considered too dangerous to walk. Aggressive, faceless women wearing faded burkas and accompanied by soiled children beg for money. One outstretched hand quickly becomes ten when street children discover a "live one." It is very uncomfortable being surrounded by children jockeying for position to be among the chosen. Raymond always rescued me when the pushing and shoving bordered on violent.

A Chicken Street Seven Eleven

A sign reading "No weapons allowed" was posted on the wall in the entrance to our hotel lobby. They needed a sign to keep weapons out of the lobby! Their only bellman, Amir, carried our bag two flights up to a room that reeked from decades of abuse, neglect and decay. He worked for the hotel twelve hours a day, six days a week. He also taught history in the afternoon at a university in Kabul, but he made more money as a bellman than he earned as a history professor.

We often caught him watching American cartoons on a very small black and white TV in the breakfast room. It had been a long time since I'd seen a rabbit ear antenna. He was as animated as the cartoon characters.

His wife and children lived too far away for him to go home at night, so he visited his family on Fridays. He was "fortunate". He had two jobs while others had none, but his children lived most of their lives without their father.

Amir, bellman and history professor

Upon arriving in our room, we drew the curtains closed to avoid being observed from the street. All three deadbolt locks on the room's thick battered metal door were engaged at all times. I never go out at night nor do most Afghans.

I ate canned chili and hamburgers cooked on hot plates by a friendly American whose name in Afghanistan was not likely the one his parents had given him. We had absolutely nothing in common but quickly became friends. I wanted to know but didn't ask, "How does an American, whose life is constantly in danger, end up working as a chef in a run-down Afghan hotel serving canned chili and hamburgers cooked on a hot plate?" We each thought the other was crazy and out of place, and we were both right.

The guests, almost entirely men, socialized at night in a bar that served alcohol. I ventured into it once, sat on a stool, and retreated within minutes. The bar was a smoke-filled zone, and the men inside had obviously been drinking well in advance of my arrival. They were the reason for the sign prohibiting guns in the lobby. They looked and acted like men who ignore signs. The cook had observed my rapid retreat and smiled knowingly as I returned to his counter and ordered fries.

Upon returning to our room after what passed for dinner, I discovered my bed sheets were torn and repaired with large strips of duct tape. Yes, duct tape! I lay awake in the bed trying not to turn so I could avoid tearing them further. Sleep meant I'd need more duct tape. The pillow could have served as a sandbag, and the stained blanket was more dust than cloth. Later, while showering, the water backed up bringing with it feces left by prior occupants.

Most of my night was spent watching soccer and cricket games on the room's small black and white TV. I was able to watch the activities on the street through small openings in the blinds. It was the worst hotel experience of my life, and oddly the most fascinating.

First Excursion to Lalander

Our first visit to Lalander, a distance of less than twenty miles, took an hour and a half by car. Once we were off the main road we rarely exceeded twenty miles an hour. Deep ruts, large boulders and holes in the road slowed us to a crawl. Several times we were forced to pull over to allow heavily burdened trucks to descend from a nearby rock quarry.

There was an encounter on one section that was nerve-wracking. Walls on both sides, too high to scale, made the road so narrow a car couldn't turn around. A car coming in the opposite direction blocked our way, and a standoff ensued. Raymond got out of our car, as did passengers in the other, to argue their right of way claims. Whoever lost would have to back up a considerable distance before there would be enough room for the other to pass. There are no rules of the road. At least none that I have observed.

This was my first experience watching Afghans argue. Volume, hand and arm gestures can be the decisive factors in winning a dispute. I was taught to keep my arms at my side and voice low. For me, shouting and raised fists are precursors to a fight. What would I do if Raymond was attacked? That dilemma wasn't hard to resolve. I would be of no help. I locked the car doors. It turns out Afghans are just more animated and forceful in pressing a point. I've yet to see Afghans fight. Raymond prevailed, they gave way and he wasn't aware I'd locked the doors.

My primary concern was that we were in the middle of a kidnapping with me as the prize. Being in the wrong place at the wrong time when a terrorist attack occurs is one risk, but the risk of kidnapping is greater. Kidnappings are far more prevalent than terrorist attacks. I kept looking behind to see whether a car had blocked our way out. I slumped down and stared straight ahead, conscious of the fact that to some my worth lies in the ransom I would command, which, in all likelihood, wouldn't meet their expectations.

Several minutes later we stopped to climb atop an abandoned Russian tank sitting alongside the road. This tank had been stripped of everything valuable, serving only as a bleak reminder of the devastation of war. I was reminded of my army basic training days in Fort Benning, Georgia. The sound of an approaching tank is terrifying—loud clanking metal treads clawing the ground and running over all obstacles in their way. I imagined how frightened the villagers must have felt when a tank turned their way and started firing at their homes.

Before reaching Lalander, we had to get out of the car and push it up and over an incline that was too steep and rocky for it to climb. The tires spun over dirt and gravel. I discovered too late that pushing from behind a spinning tire is not where you want to be. Fortunately, a few sheepherders who were passing by came to our aid.

INSTALL IT AND THEY WILL COME
Our first stop in Lalander was to visit the school we'd funded. I was sent a photo of the school before our visit which I'd shown to several

adults before taking it to Happy Valley Elementary School in Lafayette, California to share with students who had helped raise funds for the cause. Within fifteen seconds of seeing the photo, a fourth grader asked something that no one else had asked, "Where are the swings?" There weren't any. He noticed what no adult had, including me. The school had no playground equipment.

We were told that Central Asia Institute had promised to provide playground equipment, but "it hadn't arrived." Seeing that a school nearby also had no equipment, we immediately ordered and installed swings, monkey bars, a seesaw, and a slide. Three days after they were installed enrollment increased by ten students.

It takes so little to bring joy into their lives.

When I returned to the school six months later, a young Afghan student stood in the classroom and thanked me, adding, "We'd like to play soccer." There were no soccer fields in the entire valley. We subsequently paid the cost of having a bulldozer level the land adjoining the school, installed two goal posts, bought soccer balls, and hired a soccer coach. TIE's first of five soccer programs was launched. The total cost of the first field and soccer program was seven hundred dollars plus fifty dollars per month for the coach.

Afghan students are not required by law to go to school. Installing playground equipment and adding soccer programs is a very inexpensive way to increase enrollment and reduce absenteeism. Schools become fun places to be.

MONEY BUYS EQUALITY

Before my first visit to Afghanistan, a highly regarded Afghan women's rights activist from Kabul, Surya Parlika, had dinner at my house. She'd been arrested and imprisoned by the Taliban when they governed Kabul for organizing home classes for girls. I asked her what I should say to encourage fathers to allow their daughters to go to school. Should I argue that the first word in the Koran is "Read", and nowhere in the Koran is there any suggestion that this directive is "for boys only?" Should I argue fundamental fairness? After a long pause, Surya responded, "Tell them educated women will bring more money to their family."

While in Lalander, I informed a group of Afghan fathers that Americans who have college degrees earn, on average, one million dollars more, during their lifetimes, than those who don't. I told them what Surya recommended, their daughters, if educated, could produce income for their family. Five days later the school headmaster told me twenty-eight new students had enrolled in his school following our meeting. Unfortunately, all were boys. I was advised that most fathers, living in Lalander who weren't allowing their daughters to go to school, were afraid of what the Taliban might do to them.

No Shoes No School

While in the village, we learned there were children in Lalander not attending school due to the condition of their footwear or lack thereof. One boy stayed home because he would be required to wear his mother's shoes to school. He didn't own a pair and was too embarrassed to let others know. The problem was solved when we bought twenty-five pairs of shoes at a total cost of three hundred seventy-five dollars—only fifteen dollars per child!

Where are the Women?

All of the meetings held in the village consisted of men only. We were able to meet with five women from Lalander in our office in Kabul hoping that they would be able to establish a women's *shura* (council). It was, as far as I know, the first attempt in the village to organize the women and give them a voice. That was their first and last meeting.

For the first time in my life I encountered women whose lives were completely controlled by men and who were depressed by and resigned to their fate. I knew there was an issue over educating girls and assumed it would be resolved once the Taliban were defeated. The Taliban are not, however, the only impediment to achieving equal rights for women. There is an ancient cultural tradition, mostly adhered to within rural Afghan homes, that allows women to be treated as inferior and subservient to men.

No Going Back

By the end of 2005, my commitment had grown well beyond financing the construction of a school. I had read about our involvement in Afghanistan, met the people, viewed the conditions and was deeply troubled by the injustices inflicted on powerless women. I also discovered what many of you already know. Coming to the aid of others produces life's most rewarding moments. By the end of 2005, it simply wasn't possible to return to the life I had led before. I was addicted to helping and had found a village where I could.

CHAPTER 5

Events in 2006
Never Assume—Verify

❖ ❖ ❖

THE TWO MAIN GUIDING PRINCIPLES in providing humanitarian aid are transparency and verifiability. When visiting Lalander last year, Raymond and I were shown a terraced and barren hillside that had once been covered with fruit trees. Every tree was gone, destroyed during the ten-year war waged against Russian "occupiers."

Lalander is unfortunately within rocket range of Kabul. The mujahideen, under the leadership of warlord Gulbuddin Hekmartyr, fired thousands of rockets into Kabul from Lalander during Russia's occupation. In retaliation the Russians came to Lalander, destroyed homes and aqueduct systems, and planted land mines. Restoring water and orchards to the valley was very high on Lalander's wish list.

A natural spring was located a long way from the barren hillside. In 2005, TIE funded the building of a trench to bring water from the spring to the hillside so fruit trees could be replanted. Raymond and I crossed a small stream and climbed over several steep hills in rocky tilled soil to verify whether the work had been done. Our Afghan hosts kept saying the spring was "close." This was true only once—the fifth time I asked. "Close" for Afghan farmers is very far by my standards. It was embarrassing for me and comical for them how often I had to stop and rest before reaching the spring.

23

We had been led to believe that the trench had been finished. It hadn't. The contractor had been paid and he wasn't coming back. An eighteen-thousand-dollar irrigation project fell short by fifty yards because it needed another six hundred dollars' worth of concrete! We bought the additional concrete and the villagers finished the job.

That day I learned a valuable lesson. Everything, we are told, must be verified by someone who can be trusted. Had we not taken the hike, we would never have known it wasn't finished and the hillside still wouldn't be farmable.

Destroy the aqueducts and destroy the farmers.

LUNCH AT AFGHANADDIN'S

Immediately following our inspection, one of Lalander's *maliks* (village leaders), Afghanaddin, insisted we stay for lunch. Culturally, refusing a meal invitation particularly by a *malik*, can be taken as an insult. As we approached Afghannadin's home his wife, working in their yard, saw us coming and ran inside. She was the first and only woman I saw in Lalander during our entire visit. She did not reappear. Shielding girls and women from the outside world is a matter of custom and security which makes it extremely difficult to know how women are being treated inside their homes.

We filed into a dimly lit room and took seats on a beautiful oriental carpet. There were a few pillows scattered around and they gave me two—one to sit on and one for my back. There were not enough for everyone so I offered one of mine to a man sitting next to me who had none. He insisted I use both. Afghans are well known for their hospitality—taking pride in welcoming, feeding, and making guests comfortable. By custom they are also obligated to protect guests.

I folded my legs into a yoga position until my muscles could stretch no more. Noticing my discomfort, men sitting next to me moved so that I could extend my limbs. I looked out of place which of course, I was. Note to travelers: Head for a corner if asked to sit on the floor. There is more legroom, and corner walls will provide bracing for your back.

Afghannadin's eldest son, followed by two younger brothers, brought in a well-worn, very large, dented silver teapot and began pouring water over guests' outstretched hands, one by one. The water cascaded off hands most, but not all, landing into a pan held by the second boy. The third and youngest followed holding out a tray with small folded cloth towels.

This process passes for cleansing, but our hands were far from clean. The water was cold, there was no soap, and there weren't enough hand towels to go around for everyone. When it was my turn, the towels had all been used by others. I found a small, dry area on the edge of one and carefully dried my hands with it. The next guest wasn't so fortunate.

There was a knife, fork, and spoon near my plate. Everyone around me began eating with their fingers. I fully intended to adopt the "when in Rome" approach until I realized they were sharing plates of food. Fingers dove into a mound of rice and scooped a load that was then guided into a mouth. The fingers then returned for more.

Fingers washed without soap in cold water, dried with wet communal towels, were now delivering saliva back to shared plates of food. From that moment on, I spoon out my portion from the plates before anyone dives in. Once fingers go in, I'm out!

This was also the day I stopped eating Afghan salads and raw vegetables. During our walkabout I stepped over human feces in a field and was advised that some Afghan farmers use human waste as fertilizer. My advice to all travelers wherever you go is this: Imodium. Don't leave home without it!

Finger food is everything on a plate.

MICROCREDIT FINANCING
Microfinancing, making small loans to the poor, attacks poverty one borrower at a time. It's a Nobel prize winning strategy, and justifiably

so. Donors prefer a hand up over a hand out approach to aid, as do the poor.

We first began making loans to the villagers in Lalander last year. Two hundred dollar loans were made to each of forty-five borrowers selected by their leaders. They were payable in one year and bore no interest. Borrowers were told their repayment records would support larger loans in the future and this was their opportunity to prove themselves credit worthy.

The interest charged by microcredit lenders varies. Rates of twenty percent per annum and more are not uncommon. Had we charged this rate on a two-hundred-dollar loan, borrowers would have been obligated to pay interest of forty dollars. That would have created two problems. First, the Koran forbids lenders from charging interest. Second, we would have been perceived as profiteers charging too much to people living in what was then the fifth poorest country in the world. Day laborers were making only six dollars a day. The income we would have generated wasn't worth the bad will it could have incurred.

Our plan was to eventually turn the loan program over to the village *shuras* (councils) to administer. Villages would then have microcredit loan programs administered by people they chose and they would decide whether or not to charge interest. By not charging interest, we could remain "good guys," compliant with Islamic law. Incidentally, loans made to Muslims often do not charge "interest." Borrowers are charged "service fees." This distinction has been made so lenders could appear compliant with Islamic law.

HIGH DRAMA

Not all of the loans we made this trip went smoothly. There weren't enough funds for every family living in Lalander so the *maliks* were asked to select borrowers based upon need and credit worthiness. Malik Weiss provided us with fifteen names and requested that we make the loans personally in the village. When we arrived, we were led to a beautiful fruit orchard where several carpets had been laid on the ground. More than forty men were present—borrowers and onlookers, I thought. Out came the tea and speeches.

A borrower along with two guarantors and Malik Weiss were required to sign a written loan agreement which most of the men couldn't read. All but a few couldn't write their names instead using their thumbprints. What's the point of having a contract that borrowers can't read acknowledged by thumbprints no one can check? It's better than relying on memories with selective or no recall. I knew then that we wouldn't be able to enforce the notes but also thought that being repaid wasn't as important as giving them an opportunity to prove themselves creditworthy. The worst case was that a deserving family would end up with two hundred dollars.

Everything went well until we finished the fifteenth loan and what I assumed were onlookers realized we were leaving. They had not been told there would be only fifteen, something we had assumed Malik Weiss would convey before we arrived. Two young Afghan men began shouting, . waving their fists, and arguing with others who took up their challenge. One who could not be silenced shouted, "If everyone doesn't get a loan, no one should." Four borrowers approached me, threw their two one hundred dollar bills at my feet and walked away. Everyone was urged to do the same.

Whalid Osman, an Afghan living in the United States whom I'd met in Kabul, had accompanied us to the village to take photos. He pulled me aside and told me that we should leave immediately. He was concerned for our safety and justifiably so. We couldn't be certain the men's anger wouldn't be directed at us. We were a long way from our car and had no protection other than what the villagers might provide. I was frightened by the intensity of the scene that was unfolding but didn't want to run.

I asked to speak to the most vociferous of the malcontents. We sat down, legs folded, face to face, on the carpet—a good position to be in. He would have difficulty striking me with any force while seated. I explained what had happened including my discussion with Malik Weiss, told him I understood his point of view. I offered to take back the money if that is what they decided. There simply wasn't enough money to make every family in the village a loan. I shared with him the American idiom, "money doesn't grow on trees." His demeanor changed from violent to nonviolent immediately.

After we had spoken for several minutes, I asked him how many were present who hadn't received a loan. He pointed out five including himself. I assumed there would be more. An extra thousand dollars would get us safely out of the village, a small price to pay. I had an extra thousand dollars that hadn't been allocated.

Even after I agreed to fund an additional five loans, however, he continued to argue with Maiwand, one of our program directors. I couldn't understand what they were saying, but I saw little purpose in their shouting at each other. I interrupted and asked him why he was still arguing. I said, "There's one thing I learned as a lawyer in court. When you've won the argument, stop talking." He laughed and quit arguing—crisis over. He was transformed from potential enemy to friend. Every time I saw him after that day he would wave and place his hand over his heart, a gesture I receive from every Afghan who learns why I am in Afghanistan.

After the additional loans were made, more men came forward, complaining that they hadn't received theirs. They were waved off by Malik Weiss. To this day, I don't know whether the rebellion had been staged and coordinated with Malik Weiss. He had known there would be fifteen loans and had left me hanging until I had made twenty. After that, he had stepped in and they'd backed away immediately. Why hadn't he stepped in earlier? If the rebellion had been staged, they'd played me beautifully.

Before leaving, I made a total of forty-five loans, all to men. Direct access to women while in Lalander wasn't allowed.

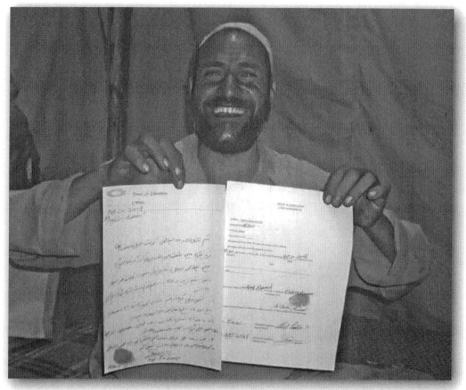

Microcredit loans—will men ever learn?

THREE HUNDRED SHEEP

This year, of the loans made last year, five were repaid and forty were not. One of the differences between most microcredit loans and ours was that we didn't restrict the use of funds. Everyone was handed two one hundred dollar bills and could spend them however he chose.

Rather than abandon micro-financing entirely, we did two things this year. First, we announced that we would not make any more loans to people living in Lalander until last year's were repaid. Instead, we worked with villages located near Lalander. Second, we did not provide cash loans. We bought three hundred sheep, and each borrower received five by signing an interest-free, two-hundred-dollar promissory note due and payable in one year.

A representative from the borrowers was invited and present when we bought the sheep. That way there would be no question as to what we'd paid. Trust is almost impossible to receive or give where people struggle to survive from day to day. Almost every Afghan in Afghanistan tells me not to trust Afghans. For us to gain their trust, it was important that they be given an opportunity to verify the cost of the sheep.

Raymond and I spent three days purchasing sheep in an open stockyard easily the size of ten football fields. By the end, we looked and smelled worse than the animals. Thousands of sheep, cattle, donkeys, horses, and camels huddled in small groups awaiting their fate. Owners with long sticks and whips prevented any of the animals' attempt to flee. Young children wandered through collecting animal droppings by hand to sell as fertilizer. I baked inside a Toyota van in hundred-degree heat while Raymond roamed throughout the stockyard purchasing sheep.

I stayed in the Toyota, out of sight, for security reasons and to avoid making Raymond's negotiations more difficult. If the sellers had known he was purchasing the animals on behalf of an American organization, their asking price would have doubled. Negotiations were friendly, loud and animated. Raymond used the "walk-away" negotiation strategy several times, as did sellers. All sales were concluded with an embrace or handshake regardless of how contentious the negotiations had been. Raymond has mastered the skill of intense negotiations while remaining friends.

The sheep were packed shoulder to shoulder into pickup trucks and driven to a site where the borrowers, who had been chosen by their *maliks* waited. We turned distribution over to the *maliks*. They adopted a very simple allocation policy: take what you're offered or get out of the line. Many complained but no one left the line.

Raymond bargains for 300 sheep in two days!

THE RESULTS ARE IN

During our two-year experiment with microcredit loans, we were able to lend to ten women and eighty-five men. Five men who had repaid their initial two-hundred-dollar loan were then loaned four hundred each. None repaid their second loan. Five of the ten women who received sheep repaid their loans. I suspect that the women who didn't were prevented by the men heading their households.

Our payback rate was therefore fifty percent for women and zero for men. We learned what other microcredit lenders have discovered throughout the world: women repay their loans and men give excuses. Of the microcredit loans made by Grameen Bank, the industry leader, ninety-four percent are made to women. Worldwide, men continue to prove they are not creditworthy. Women, however, are!

ATTEMPT TO PARTNER WITH A MICROCREDIT ORGANIZATION

Efforts to partner with a microcredit organization in Kabul proved unsuccessful. We tried. Without bothering to give anyone notice, a loan officer working for one microcredit organization failed to show for two prearranged orientation meetings. We had assembled several women on two occasions to learn about their financing program. The meetings' time and place had been arranged over a week in advance.

After the second missed appointment, the loan officer scheduled to appear at both meetings told our program director she was too busy. Why didn't she tell him that when the appointments were made? Why didn't she call the day before both appointments to let us know she wouldn't be able to attend? We could have notified those who planned to be there that the meetings were cancelled. Instead, she just failed to appear. The poor are too often subjected to program administrators who have no respect for others' time. They should be disciplined the first time it happens and fired the second.

The unwillingness of aid organizations to coordinate and cooperate with one another is frustrating. Lack of cooperation leads to the failure of organizations to share valuable information and also to avoid duplication of effort. So much more could be accomplished if they made a point of working together. We haven't given up on microcredit financing. We just haven't found a way to provide it ourselves or been able to coordinate with an organization that does.

Profiting from Microfinancing

As a side note, I am personally troubled by microcredit financing ventures sold as a "good investment." I do understand the need to charge enough interest to make a micro- credit financing program self-sustaining; however, when generating an attractive return to investors becomes part of the equation, interest rates charged to borrowers must be significantly higher.

Potential investors in a micro-credit program should be required to spend a week in the field making loans. Several of them will, I believe, be transformed from investors to donors, or at least lower the rate of return they require to invest. Face to face encounters with people qualifying for microcredit loans are life-altering. I know—I've had eighty-five.

Cash is Bulky

On my first trip to Kabul in 2006, I carried forty thousand dollars in cash with me. I didn't know anyone I could wire funds to in Kabul who could be trusted with that much money, and I was afraid a Western Union transfer that size would get lost at the other end. I needed money to make the final payment for the irrigation project, to make more microcredit loans and to buy fruit trees.

I wore a money belt, socks with zipper compartments, three money pouches strapped under my shirt and cargo pants with hundred dollar bills in every pocket. Try sleeping on a plane with forty thousand dollars of bulges.

I couldn't disclose how much I was carrying; ten thousand dollars was the limit allowed by law. If searched at the airport, I'd be arrested but at least there would be several officials aware of my arrest. I felt confident we could convince them I wasn't a drug dealer. What I didn't know is whether they'd confiscate thirty thousand dollars and leave me with ten.

There was no way for me get money to Afghanistan other than sneak it through customs. I just kept walking, smiling and saying *Salaam Alaikum* (Hello) to every customs officer who looked my way. We, the money, Raymond, and I made it through. Today I wire money and sleep well on the plane.

A Time to Plant

We had decided to buy small fruit trees, known as cuttings, for the farmers living in the valley. Farmers were given sixty cuttings, an amount we were told was the maximum that should be planted on a *jerib* (half acre). They were given a choice of fruit. Seventy percent chose apricot and thirty percent chose apple. The cuttings averaged one dollar and twenty-five cents each. In 2006 we were able to buy twelve thousand eight hundred and ninety-one. This was made possible by a fundraising drive held at Corte Madera school in Portola Valley, California, organized by a student, Aaron Ebert. They raised ten thousand dollars.

A farmer living in Lalander owned a tree farm in the valley that had six thousand trees. We bought every tree he had—He was one happy farmer! The balance was purchased from a family who owned five nurseries in Kabul. One of their sons told me they had eighty thousand cuttings. I asked him how many other organizations were buying cuttings from them for the farmers. There is a two to three-week window in the spring when they must be transplanted. We were at the end of that window. We were the only one buying from his family. No one knew of anyone else supplying cuttings to the farmers.

I was astounded to learn we were alone in providing farmers with fruit trees. Why? One objective in Afghanistan is to reduce the production of opium. Transplanted cuttings will not produce commercial quantities of fruit for four to five years. An Afghan farmer can buy and plant cuttings that won't bear significant quantities of fruit for four to five years or invest in poppy seeds, get two crops per year and require less water to grow. Income now or later—what would a farmer struggling to survive do?

We supplied more cuttings in 2007, bringing the total to over twenty-two thousand. With an average cost of one dollar and twenty-five cents per cutting and each farmer receiving sixty cuttings, the cost per farmer is seventy-five dollars. We were able to assist well over three thousand five hundred farming families in restoring fruit trees that had died as a result of the battles fought in their area.

With an average Afghan family having ten members that becomes thirty-five thousand Afghans who know we care. The United States is not in Afghanistan to win hearts and minds. But, I can't help but compare what TIE has accomplished with so little to offset the damage done by misdirected bullets, drones and bombs.

Fruit trees are heavy to a donkey, but they lighten a family's load.

CHAPTER 6

Events in 2007
March Newsletters
from Kabul

❖ ❖ ❖

I'M WRITING FROM THE AFGHANS for Tomorrow guesthouse in Kabul where eight guests are sharing one bathroom. After only two days, my hearing has adapted to the point where I am able to hear the bathroom door open fifty feet away through our bedroom wall, an evolutionary adaptation supporting Darwin's theory of "survival of the fittest."

While waiting to start my bathroom sprint, I have subconsciously compared the bathroom time needs of women and men. The ratio is two to one. The solution to waiting is to be the first, something everyone knows. My fellow sprinters have been rising earlier and earlier each day pretending we're not.

I met with the leader of the *Shura* (governing council) of the Char Asiab District. He represents 70,000 villagers, 3,000 of whom live in Lalander. He is 100% supportive of TIE's work and visited Lalander several times last year to express this support. One issue he decided to address personally is the education of girls. That takes courage. In southern Afghanistan, the Taliban have destroyed girls' schools, and taken lives over this issue.

While enrollment has continued to rise since the school TIE financed opened in March 2005, the ratio of boys to girls is three to one. We were able to partially address this problem this past winter by providing four in-home classes that over 100 women and girls attended. That's what we can do, support Afghans on the frontline from the safety of our homes. Theirs is the greater burden.

THE CIRCUS COMES TO TOWN

It is the evening after this morning's big event, the circus performing in Lalander. Afghan Mobile Mini Circus for children (MMCC), one of the best schools for children in Kabul, agreed to bring performers and a stage if we would provide transportation. No problem I thought—we would just call a bus company. But, there are no bus companies; neither is there anyone to call to arrange transportation.

Raymond hit the streets yesterday and flagged down privately owned buses loaded with passengers and weaving through nightmare traffic. He negotiated with drivers while they drove.

After six hours, he returned without having had a single bus agree to drive to Lalander. The village was, according to the drivers, "too far" and "too dangerous." Moreover, the dirt road leading to Lalander from the paved street takes a heavy toll on vehicle suspension systems and tires. We went to bed last night knowing that the circus "coming to Lalander" might not occur today or ever.

Undaunted, Raymond renewed his search this morning at 5:00 a.m. Three and a half hours later, three buses appeared at the MMCC school to load up. By the time they loaded the equipment and corralled the performers, the departure time was delayed by two hours. The total cost per bus to drive to Lalander, wait throughout the performances and meal that followed, and return to Kabul—a total elapsed time of six hours—was forty dollars. But, arrive the circus did, with acrobats, jugglers, singers, and comedians, three hours late.

Before they arrived, I visited a nearby school not funded by TIE. Last year there were no girls enrolled in that school. In exchange for our agreeing to provide financial assistance, we were assured that girls would attend this year. There were girls in one of the classrooms.

I was very pleased to have broken through the boys only barrier. One class with girls was a start. My excitement was dashed later when Raymond learned they had been brought to the school for my benefit. They would be reassembled if I returned. The truth is girls are still not attending that school. I had been misled.

One comedy sketch displayed a large banner featuring explosive devices. The comedians sang, danced, and pointed at several of the devices, warning the children not to touch or go near any of them. The sketch was funny. The subject was not. I was advised that there is an average of one hundred land mine accidents in Afghanistan per month. Most of the injuries and deaths involve children inadvertently playing in or straying into mine fields.

A great time was had by all. Well, almost all. Thirty minutes before the show began, I realized that the audience included only twelve young girls and not a single woman, except one sitting with a young child high on a hill overlooking and behind the stage. She and her child never joined the audience and received no food. To avoid upsetting the villagers and putting anyone at risk, MMCC didn't bring any female performers either.

Later that day, I met with a small group of women and asked them why women and more girls hadn't attended. "Things are different here," was the response, delivered as a statement of fact without emotion or comment. Those present seemed resigned to things being "different" including being excluded from the only time the circus would come to town.

I chose not to follow up with questions I would have liked to ask her. I am an American and a guest. An open conversation about women's rights is perceived by some as meddling in their lives, "none of my business." Taliban extremists do not want foreigners advocating women's rights and have been known to harm those who have. At this moment in time, I had to be content with the answer, "things are different."

SECURITY PROTECTION

I'm frequently asked whether we have security protection when visiting villages? We never request bodyguards, though they are offered and would be provided if we asked. It seems to me that our message, "We're friends and here to help," would be undermined if we were accompanied by guards holding AK-47s. On circus day, because word of the event had spread throughout the valley, there were armed men, who were never far from my side. Afghan guards holding AK-47s are both reassuring and frightening. There's always the risk that their guns would be turned on us.

The circus performers devote time to a serious subject: landmines.

First the circus then food. A great day but not for all.

NOT WHAT I'D ENVISIONED

Circus day was troubling. They'd lied to us about girls being in the school. The *shura's* leader's support of educating girls had had no discernable impact. No women and only a few girls had been allowed to watch the performers, and all female performers had been left home. I had A-K 47s follow me throughout the day. I had imagined a village picnic with free food and entertainment, enjoyed by all.

I was awakened to the disturbing knowledge that only twenty miles from Kabul, women are living their lives behind high walls and locked doors, not allowed to leave without permission or go out without being accompanied by a man. They seem resigned to their station in life, something my daughter would never be.

After all we had done, they lied to me about girls being in school and went so far as to stage their presence. I thought about giving up and have several times since. Every time I have the internal debate about quitting, I reach the same conclusion. Our support of education is too important to the future of Afghan girls and women to stop. We cannot win the war for gender equality. We can win individual battles, and that is enough.

Rats!

I learned today that rats are killing many of the fruit trees that had been planted last year. The problem with poisons is that they kill all animals, not just rats. Farmers dig holes in the ground near the base of a tree and insert cans filled half way with water. Rats fall in and drown. But the rats are winning. A female can reproduce up to six times a year with litters averaging from four to eight pups each.

I remember as a child, living in Pocatello, Idaho that my father was an excellent hunter. One reason he was a "good shot" is that when he was a child, the city had a rabbit infestation problem in its surrounding hills. The city rewarded whoever killed rabbits a bounty for each rabbit they killed. My father, unlike me, didn't have or need a paper route.

I went rabbit hunting a few times with my father and later ended up on a rifle team as a result. Rabbits, to their detriment, often stop and sit up when they hear a sound. Whistling works best. The best part of hunting as a child was the stop at the donut shop before the hunt began.

I told Raymond about the reward system and agreed to do the same for rats. We offered to pay five cents for every rat killed. One problem was they didn't have low caliber guns. So, we bought and distributed ten high-powered pellet guns and gave each recipient three thousand pellets.

We bought them at a gun stall in downtown Kabul. The gun venders were located in the middle of a large open market. Raymond and I walked briskly through the crowds, bought the guns and retreated as quickly as we could. We must always assume someone might kidnap, harm, or kill us, wherever we go.

When Raymond explained the reward to those receiving a gun and pellets, all they did was laugh. I should have known. Who wants to bring in dead rats? And, who would be willing to have the hundreds if not thousands of rats brought to their home for payment? The bounty for rats program failed before it started. Now, if the problem had only been rabbits...

Raymond checks out a pellet gun in one of hundreds of gun stalls.

CHAPTER 7

Events in 2008
Attacks on the Rise

❖   ❖   ❖

ATTACKS ON AFGHAN SCHOOLS AND educators teaching girls are increasing. During the night, notes are left by the Taliban on household doors threatening harm to families allowing their daughters to go to school.

In response to these threats, TIE agreed to finance classes taught in homes within small villages. They are safer to attend. Strangers who might pose a threat are easily identified. Peer pressure also has an impact on enrollment. It's much more difficult to not allow a girl to attend classes when her friends are attending.

Most news reports fail to note that the vast majority of Afghans want their daughters to be educated, and the number is growing. Each year, it becomes easier for girls to take our classes and go to schools near where they live. The tide is turning, albeit very slowly.

Waiting for school to open.

April Report from Kabul
Getting Through the Airport

Last Friday, I arrived at Kabul airport to be greeted by twice the security we've previously experienced. While I was standing in line to clear customs, a guard approached intending to escort me to the front of the line. I declined, having learned previously that this leads to a relentless and open request for money and to justifiable resentment by others waiting in line. It is common practice, however, for women to be escorted or go to the front of the line as this minimizes their contact with men.

Retrieving my luggage from the carousel was a survival of the fittest exercise. Four baggage handlers decided they would carry my luggage. They fought and argued among themselves until three prevailed, one for each bag. I pointed to a luggage cart and my baggage and held up one finger, trying to convey that I needed only one porter. That gesture succeeded in reducing the number from three to two.

For security reasons, the parking for passenger pickup is several blocks and three checkpoints away from the terminal. The two baggage handlers passed me off to another when we got outside the airport building insisting that they were not allowed to go further. That wasn't true, and I knew it. In the past handlers have taken me all the way to the pickup zone.

Not wanting to create an "ugly American" scene and realizing how important tips are to them, I went along with their maneuvering. A few extra dollars wouldn't hurt me and would make a major difference in their lives. Tipping is not only a way to reward services rendered. Tipping is also a way of sharing wealth with no middleman fees.

I gave each of them two dollars and they both acted as if it wasn't enough. Day laborers earn eight dollars a day. Two dollars each was plenty, particularly considering I didn't need two baggage handlers and they were forcing me to use a third. Ingrates they weren't...just desperate.

MORE GUNS

The doubling of security at the airport and in Kabul was to control and protect crowds gathering in recognition of the mujahideen's successful seizure and recovery of Kabul from the Russians, which is celebrated every year. Our hotel, the Intercontinental, had at least thirty armed men at the three checkpoints leading to the entrance. Ironically, the more security there is at the hotel, the less secure I feel. When they beef up security it's because the risk of attack is greater. They are on greater alert, and consequently so am I.

Redistributing Our Stuff

TIE's first shipment to Afghanistan through the Denton program—5,541 pounds of clothing, household and school supplies, games, soccer balls and shoes—arrived in time for Raymond and me to participate in a distribution. Administered by USAID and the military, the Denton Program allows humanitarian aid to be shipped on military aircraft for free when there is room.

Reasonable men and women disagree over the need to redistribute wealth, but there is little opposition to the redistribution of things we no longer need. If there is one thing we have enough of in this country, it's stuff.

Our First Distributions

We had established two distribution days, which were by invitation only. Our teachers and village leaders select the poorest families in their village—an extremely difficult and undesirable task. No one wants to decide who will and will not be allowed to participate. After all, who wouldn't consider themselves deserving in the fifth poorest country in the world.

On the first day, only fathers and sons came to the distribution explaining, "It's difficult for women." It's "difficult" only because men determine when, how often and how long women can leave their homes. We decided to see just how difficult it would be.

We sent word to the village that on the following day we would allow only mothers and their young children to attend. They could be accompanied by a few men for security reasons, but this time the men were advised to remain home. It was entirely possible no one would come.

Sixty women, girls, and young boys arrived accompanied by Afghannadin, one of Lalander's leaders, and a few men he had chosen. We had prevailed! The things we no longer need are that valuable to them!

Laid out on tarps, the clothing was separated into piles for men, women, boys, girls, and infants. Concerned that there would be fighting if everyone was allowed to charge the piles at the same time, we divided the women into three groups of twenty each.

Raymond explained to everyone that each group would have five minutes to make selections. Within three minutes after the first group began, the others couldn't restrain themselves and joined in. The "better stuff" was going fast. Blankets were the most sought after items. Blankets are literally life-savers during the winter months. We failed to explain to them that we had withheld boxes of clothing that would be emptied and added to the piles after each group took its turn.

For years I have seen news reports of doors opening at shopping malls in the United States on sale days and the ensuing struggles over "mark downs." I was absolutely certain there would be pushing, shoving, and fighting over what lay on the ground. I was wrong.

When two women lifted up a down ski jacket at the same time each holding onto a sleeve, I expected a tug of war would begin. There were no tugs only pushes as each insisted that the other take the jacket. Quickly resolving the issue, they turned away to make more selections. Not one fight or argument erupted the entire time. Others before self was the guiding principle of the day, a value I've often observed in Afghanistan.

We now minimize the number of men who participate in distributions. Women are much better at picking clothes for their families and don't plan to sell what they select. Our program directors, Maiwand and Basir, have stepped in several times to stop men from grabbing whatever they could, because we can tell from their behavior they would head straight to the bazaar. Afghan women have, on more than one occasion, proven themselves to be more responsible, considerate, and trustworthy than the men. Afghan women clearly hold up more than half Afghanistan's sky.

From our homes to theirs.

He's not crazy about the hat. But, he will be warm.

CAMERAS NOT WELCOME

Half of the women wore the traditional light blue burqa while the rest covered their heads with a scarf. When I began taking photographs, all but a few fled out of range, turned away, or covered their faces. Only the most brazen would allow a photograph and only after us talking to them.

We explained how important it was that we be able to prove to people in the United States that their donations were going where intended. A few agreed to pose for photos. Most hid from the lens. They were obviously uncomfortable. One asked us to promise her photograph would not be shown in Afghanistan. Everyone in Afghanistan, including us, wants to stay far below the radar. The emotional lift that comes when landing in San Francisco upon returning home is immediate and strong.

OCTOBER REPORT FROM KABUL
MEETING WITH THE GOVERNOR

I met with the governor of the Char Asiab District in his home. During the meeting, three of his sons were summoned and joined our discussion while two of his younger daughters peered in from the outside through a dusty, streaked and cracked windowpane. They giggled and disappeared when I looked their way, and I realized that it was best if I ignored their presence. That way they could stare and listen without having to hide from my view. Neither was invited to join us, nor was I introduced to them or his wife despite her being in the house.

One of subjects discussed with the governor was family planning. I explained to him that currently the average Afghan family has eight children and with that birth rate, Afghanistan's population would double from thirty million to sixty million in twenty years. Afghanistan is the fifth poorest country in the world with an annual per capita income of

$300. Adding another thirty million people in twenty years, according to projections, would not be sustainable. He was aware of the problem, but not the statistics or consequences.

I asked whether the leaders within his district would be receptive to a family planning program. Founded in 1976, Marie Stopes International provides a number of reproductive services in thirty-seven countries, one of which is family planning. I had offered to pay the cost of Marie Stopes International training ten women to provide health care services in his district, including family planning seminars. Prior to our meeting, its director explained how a program would be established and what it would involve.

The first step is for *mullahs* (religious leaders) affiliated with Marie Stopes International to meet with *mullahs* in the district to explain how family planning is consistent with teachings in the Koran. If the local *mullahs* approve, couples are invited to participate in counseling sessions. If the *mullahs* don't approve, it's over.

Gender segregated sessions are held enabling the men and women to express their concerns and ask questions more openly. In the afternoon the couples meet in a joint session to share and review what the two segregated groups had discussed. After the combined session each couple meets with a counselor. Ideally the process is completed before Friday. Most Afghans don't work on Fridays, and it is the day normally designated for procreation.

Family planning is not referred to as such by Marie Stopes' counselors. Instead they use "family spacing," calling upon a farmer's knowledge of crop rotation. They explain that women's bodies, like the soil, need time to recover. "Spacing" between childbirths is important for the health of mothers and children alike, and the counselors recommend "no less than three years" between births. When asked what their family planning goal is, the director said, "Reduce the number of children in a family from eight to four."

Marie Stopes counselors never tell an Afghan man that he cannot afford more children. That would be insulting and an attack on his ability to provide. I was asked who I thought would be the most difficult person to convince that a family have fewer children. It is not the husband or wife. It's the husband's mother. Mothers-in-law exercise considerable influence and control over their daughters-in-law.

The governor didn't know how the leaders in Char Asiab valley would respond. Smiling proudly, he let us know that he had two wives and eighteen children and joked (I think) that he was looking for a third wife. When I told him we would not ask him to conduct any of the seminars and he would not be on the family planning posters, his smile grew broader.

An explanation of why Afghan families are so large came from one of our teachers who brought a newborn child to our meetings with her two years in a row. When I asked why she had so many children, she smiled and said, "There isn't much to do around here"—a simple answer and true.

The meeting ended with me asking the governor to support one more program that would help Afghan men have a better understanding of American men. He could start that night by helping his two wives fix dinner and do the dishes. He laughed and said, "Afghanistan is not quite ready for democracy." Democracy and men cooking and washing dishes is an interesting word association. Perhaps there is a correlation between women acquiring the right to vote in 1920 and men spending more time in the kitchen.

"What About Me?"

Yesterday I met a young mother who stood quietly in the back of the room, a young child in her arms, during one of the classes attended by her daughter. She approached us at the end and said, "What about me? I have nothing to do all day but work. I want to learn. I have no education. I am sick. I know I am sick. I go to the doctor, and he tells me I'm not sick. I know I am sick because I am hitting my children."

This young mother was so desperate that she confessed to me and a room full of mothers and children that she was taking her isolation and depression out on her children. She didn't care what classes she took. She was willing to learn "anything." From that moment forward, our classes became open to girls and women of any age, and our teachers were advised to be proactive in inviting all women and girls to attend. We now have women in their twenties sitting alongside girls in their teens learning together. The older women are generally more motivated, learn faster, and more than willing to teach others.

What about her?

I had never before realized the importance of literacy. Reading allows the mind to travel even when a person can't, and writing enables people who might never meet to communicate. Both would open a world of ideas and information to this woman who "has nothing to do all day but work." And, if she is right about her sickness, she'll stop hurting her children.

ANOTHER SETBACK

Last winter, we provided four computers and supported after school computer classes in Lalander. Today we learned that someone from the Ministry of Education visited the school and concluded the Ministry needed the computers more than the students. He took two, leaving the teacher with sixteen students and two computers. Three steps forward and one back, I guess, is better than two forward and one back, which is how we began.

CHAPTER 8

Events in 2009
Conditions on the
Ground in Kabul

❖ ❖ ❖

NABI AND I ARRIVED IN Kabul only to discover that on the road leading to our hotel, there had been a terrorist attack the previous day. That road is riskier than others because it is a frequent route for military and government vehicles. Ironically, the safest roads are those not traveled by armored Humvees.

It is often impossible for Americans working for the State Department, USAID and NGOs to leave their compounds. Trips outside their office must be approved and are monitored by security personnel. Last year I met a lawyer who had spent two years in Kabul working for the State Department and she never left the compound during her entire stay. This is very unfortunate. Spending time with the locals is the most enjoyable part of our trips. It's also the most effective way to learn, share what we know and advocate what we believe.

There are considerably more concrete barriers and road barricades than when I first visited in 2005. It's impossible to relax while driving to destinations. Soldiers and policemen hold their automatic weapons at the ready and stare into passing cars. When I'm spotted they normally smile.

I'm clean shaven, white, make eye contact, smile and wave if they approach our car. Only a misguided, naive, idealistic and harmless American looks and behaves this way. Profiling works to my advantage; nevertheless, Basir makes sure I'm back in the hotel by sundown.

MEETING WITH VILLAGERS

Yesterday we spent several hours with leaders from the village of Farza. They asked for financial support to build a school for girls. They offered to provide the labor and requested that we provide the materials. The meeting was held at our office thereby making it our responsibility to buy everyone lunch. Our take-out food didn't meet their standards, a fact I learned after they left. Is it necessarily a bad thing for us to be viewed as cheap when it comes to entertaining guests? What isn't spent on them will go into programs.

One of the leaders brought with him a guard carrying an AK-47. Somehow I ended up sitting next to the guard. He laid the gun across his lap with the barrel pointed away from me. I found myself always keeping an eye on the gun.

During the meeting we heard a window break in an adjoining room. A neighbor had thrown a rock through the glass. Someone had been looking into the neighbor's yard from our window while his wife was outside. No one, other than me, was surprised by his action. After all, she wasn't sun-bathing. Apparently we are responsible for who is looking out our windows and what they are viewing. We'd just have to have the glass replaced.

MEETING WITH TEACHERS

We met with the twenty-nine instructors on our payroll who teach classes before and after school. We asked them to submit their wish lists and give us suggestions on how we can improve or add to our educational pro-grams. We also advised them that every teacher would receive a year-end bonus, equal to one month's salary.

The bonuses were made possible by the One Teacher to Another Fund started by Rozan Gautier of Walnut Creek, California. We promised teachers contributing to this fund that their donations would be used to increase teacher salaries. Our teachers know the source of their bonuses. They were surprised to learn they share one thing in common with their American counterparts. Both have, out of necessity, purchased supplies for their classes. Afghan teachers don't, however, receive any financial support from parents or their community; nor do their schools.

By contrast, recently I saw a sign seeking contributions from the Lafayette community for one of its school districts. The thermometer was red well beyond the halfway point, indicating they were more than halfway to their million-dollar goal.

We were informed that Taliban insurgents recently visited families in Lalander and warned them not to work or cooperate with the Afghan government. Surprisingly, nothing yet has been said about their daugh-ters attending TIE's home school classes for girls or working with TIE. Notwithstanding these warnings and the presence of the Taliban, none of our teachers have stopped teaching. If they won't stop, we won't either.

FAST TRACKING STUDENTS

During the teachers meeting, I asked whether they would like us to pro-vide courses for their better students during the winter break. The "fast track" idea got the "swift boot." I was told, "Better students are good for the slower ones who they help and motivate. Combining the two groups also creates healthy competition in the classroom."

I wasn't advocating "fast track." I just wanted to know what they thought. They believe, as many do, that all boats should rise together.

Private courses are available for those who can afford them and cost between $10 and $20 per month.

I was more successful when I asked teachers if they would be willing to take classes. They were particularly interested in the courses that would improve their teaching skills. We offered to share the cost—Only one teacher took us up on our offer. Afghan women have so many responsibilities at home there is very little time for anything else. In addition, their movements are severely restricted by custom and safety concerns. Many or most cannot go anywhere without being accompanied by a male member of the household.

COMMUNITY SUPPORT FOR EDUCATION

One of the more troubling issues we had to resolve this trip was a mounting request for pens, pencils, paper, notebooks, and other school supplies. When TIE classes were first offered in a few homes, we provided the supplies. If we hadn't, many students wouldn't have had them. At thirty dollars per student annually, in the beginning, the cost was nominal. Now that our classes enroll over five hundred students, the cost would be fifteen thousand dollars a year, which is greater than our budget for teacher salaries.

We explained to the teachers that we could not provide school supplies to every student, but we would for children whose families could not afford them. "Who would make that determination?" Farzana asked. "Parents," I replied, provoking laughter from the teachers. They knew most parents wouldn't provide their children with supplies, even if they could afford them. The teachers did not want the responsibility of deciding who would receive school supplies and who would not. They made it clear that we would be expected to provide school supplies for all or none.

The lack of parental support for schools and their children's education is something we've encountered in every village. We've come to the unfortunate conclusion that the only way for us to move them toward self-sufficiency is to gradually reduce our support.

We informed the teachers before we left that TIE could no longer afford to provide school supplies for students. They, the parents and village, would need to address that problem. We'll see what happens.

QUALITY CONTROL

A delicate issue has been brewing for over a year. Our English teacher's literacy skills aren't improving. We suggested a year ago that she take English classes during the winter break. She was aware of her limitations and agreed to take courses to improve her skills. We offered to share the cost. Before the school year began in 2010, she was asked by the villagers to step aside in favor of a more qualified teacher. She agreed without complaining. This teacher has always been more concerned about the welfare of her students than her own. The love of children above self is a quality I've often observed in teachers.

When we first began, the villagers chose the teachers we hired. Now they recommend candidates and Basir makes the final determination. This avoids friends being hired who aren't qualified. It also removes the pressure from a villager who may be expected to hire one candidate over another even if not as well qualified.

EXPANDING THE SOCCER PROGRAM

Maiwand Nemati, Raymond's brother, located land TIE will be able to lease next spring for a soccer field. Negotiations over lease terms are underway. We will fund as many soccer fields and soccer programs as we can afford. They are "no brainers"—find land, level it, and install goal posts. Throw in soccer balls and fifty dollars per month for a coach and launch a soccer program that will continue for years. It costs less than two thousand dollars the first year to add play, joy and laughter into the lives of children who have so little.

Why Can't We Work Together?

We met with staff members of the United Nations Refugee Program in a concerted effort to coordinate TIE's winter distribution of five hundred buckets of enriched rice (the equivalent of eighty-five thousand meals donated by Stop Hunger Now) and three hundred fifty large boxes of clothing, shoes, blankets and other critical donated supplies. We didn't want to distribute food and clothing to a refugee camp that would receive ample aid from other organizations.

"Astounding" best describes the lack of coordination among the entities providing aid in Afghanistan—organizations which include the State Department, USAID, ISAF, the US military, and the United Nations. The United Nations refugee organization didn't have answers to the basic questions and didn't know anyone who did. Even a list of aid organizations with contact information couldn't be provided. We had no choice but to do our own thing without knowing whether there would be duplication.

Starve them Out

Winters in Afghanistan are brutal. During the night, children freeze to death in the refugee camps in numbers no one wants to admit. One of the fathers interviewed in a camp said, "There are days when I must choose between food and firewood. I buy firewood. You can live longer without food."

Providing aid to families living in refugee camps has its detractors. Many are squatters living on land they don't own or have the right to occupy. The refugee population increases every year.

Technically most are not refugees. They are known among statisticians as IDPs or internally displaced persons. The designation refugee is reserved for displaced persons who leave their country. Hardly anyone knows the difference, and it is easier to say refugee.

Large aid organizations purportedly have been asked by the Afghan government not to provide aid to some camps in Kabul. They want the "homeless" to return home. Understandably, they won't leave if life is better where they are than where they are from. It may also be too dangerous for them to return home.

There must be a better solution to solving the homeless problem than allowing people to starve and young children to die. No one has encouraged or told us to stop helping families living in the camps. We'll confront that issue when and if it ever arises.

She calls it "home." Some want her out.

PIGS IN AFGHANISTAN!

Today we were told the schools are closed to inhibit the spread of "swine flu." Swine flu in a country where there is only one pig. Yes, one pig, named Wilbur, who is quarantined in the Kabul zoo. Lamb flu, perhaps, but certainly not swine!!

THE WAR FOR HEARTS AND MINDS

The Afghan central government and the United States are engaged with the Taliban in a war for the hearts and minds of the Afghan people. Without support from its citizens, the Taliban will succeed in overthrowing the government. I am having trouble understanding what appears to be the current hearts and minds strategy.

According to several village leaders located just outside Kabul, they receive very little support from the Afghan and United States governments. Their impression is that substantially more support is going to areas where the "Taliban are active," areas such as Helmand Province and Kandahar.

Their view is consistent with information I've obtained about programs and projects undertaken by government and non-government organizations in Afghanistan. I've tried to direct programs and projects into villages close to Kabul, and been told, by several of these organizations, they have chosen to work in "underserved areas."

Effectively, government and non-government support is now "leap-frogging" over villages close to Kabul in favor of villages where support for the central government is weaker and the Taliban are stronger. This strategy effectively rewards areas where the Taliban are gaining ground. As a result, Afghans living closest to Kabul are becoming increasingly disenchanted with the Afghan government.

The cost of applying resources to areas far from Kabul is much greater. Recently, I met with the head of an organization that will go unnamed. He explained that they were transporting computer equipment from Kabul to their office in Kandahar by car. Company policy required that the computers be insured while being transported. The cost of insurance was $10,000—a "ridiculous sum considering the value of the equipment being delivered," he said. Nonetheless, he "had no choice."

Intuitively, it seems the better strategy would be to work from the center out. Apply more resources to the villages immediately adjoining the major cities and move outward as funding permits.

Villages receiving government support are more likely to defend the government, provide valuable intelligence and defeat the Taliban themselves. As outlying villages discover the benefits of aligning themselves with the central government, they will "buy in" and be rewarded for their support. Leap-frogging increases the risk that as the Taliban advance to the capital, there won't be enough resistance.

We Had Him!!

Nabi and I had the good fortune of sharing breakfast with Gary Berntsen, author of *Jawbreaker*. Gary, a CIA operative, and a field commander in the invasion of Afghanistan in 2001, was a "go-to guy on the ground." Gary helped orchestrate the defeat of the Taliban within a few weeks of his arrival. He led the CIA's team into Tora Bora, a mountainous region near the Pakistan border. Their mission included capturing or killing Osama Bin Laden. He was flown in with a footlocker containing eleven million dollars in cash to buy whatever support he deemed necessary.

We met in the dining hall of The Green Village, a well-fortified, walled-in area with barracks built to house whoever qualified for secured housing. High walls with guard towers and mounted machine guns protected the compound. We, our vehicle and contents were searched before being allowed to enter.

Our small narrow room had two single beds, a couch and a small bathroom. The cost including cafeteria meals was one hundred twenty-five dollars a night. Fortunately, they had catsup and hot sauce. Someone had to vouch for you to get in. It was full every night we were there.

When not working, residents drink, play pool, cards and share pizzas and stories in a large community room. Nabi met several Afghan-American interpreters he knew. Rumor also had it from several sources that interpreters are earning over twelve thousand dollars per month, including those not translating in combat zones. Rumor also had it that private contracts with the US government are negotiated on a cost plus basis; therefore, the higher the cost of interpreters, the better for a contractor. Both Nabi and I were incensed to learn how much they were being paid, knowing how much that money could provide. Teachers in Afghanistan are paid one hundred fifty dollars per month.

According to Gary, "Bin Laden's retreat was blocked on three sides in Tora Bora. There was only one direction he could escape. It led to Pakistan." Gary called everyone in command in Afghanistan and in Washington D.C. requesting eight hundred troops to close the route to Pakistan. He estimated that bin Laden and one thousand of his troops were heading to Pakistan. It was the only direction they could go. His pleas for troops were denied.

Gary has a fascinating, forceful, reassuring, and aggressive personality, and is well known for his candor. It's probably why he was reassigned out of Afghanistan, shortly after the decision to not send troops was made.

Had Bin Laden been killed or captured, as Gary felt certain he would, there would have been no need for us to remain in Afghanistan. We went in to "get Bin Laden." The mission would have been accomplished, and our soldiers could have returned home.

His book, *Jawbreaker*, has many passages that were stricken by the Central Intelligence Agency. The sentences censored are blackened in the book. Even if you don't have time to read the book, flip through the pages and see how much was deemed too sensitive by the CIA.

After breakfast, Gary was on his way to visit an orphanage in Kabul he planned to help. His compassion for and desire to help Afghans is shared by every soldier I've met in Afghanistan.

CITY-WIDE SHUTDOWN

This morning we were restricted to the compound for several hours. Roads in and around Kabul were closed yesterday for security reasons. No one knew which roads had been closed or for how long. In the afternoon, a forty-minute cross-town trip took us three hours. That's three hours inhaling exhaust fumes and dust in a van without air-conditioning. On the bright side, we didn't need to worry about being kidnapped. The traffic jam precluded any possibility of a hijacking and successful getaway.

LEARNING CENTERS

Our homeschooling classes taught in villages are very popular, but living rooms proved to be too small. A small garage on Wahid's property in Qala Esfandyar was converted into a classroom two years ago at a cost of four hundred dollars; it also proved to be too small.

Wahid and his friends offered to build a larger classroom on his property. We provided the materials (four thousand eight hundred forty dollars) and entered into a ten-year rent free lease with Wahid. Wahid and his wife Zeba are passionate about educating children and are the most generous and caring partners we have had.

The new classroom is large enough to provide desks and several bookshelves. The converted garage will now be used to provide computer classes. Students no longer sit on the floor, have books in "their library" that can be checked out, and will soon be working with computers. Parents of children taking our classes have asked me more times than I can remember to please "thank the Americans" and tell them, "They are in our prayers."

The benefits of Wahid's classrooms were so compelling that we agreed to fund the construction of a classroom on Farzana's property next spring. Farzana is our most passionate, dedicated, creative, and resourceful teacher. Her living room can't hold all the children who want to take her classes.

We told her that before she marries, we want her husband to sign an agreement acknowledging and endorsing her commitment to education. She said, "As long as there are children willing to learn, I will be a teacher."

Body Language

As a footnote to this progress report, I'd like to share a reassuring observation. When I first visited classrooms several years ago, most girls avoided eye contact with me. They would look down or away if their faces weren't covered. Today, instead of bowing their heads and avoiding my glances, most seek eye contact and look directly my way. Very few faces are covered, and postures are upright reflecting pride instead of subservience. The body language is completely different than it was when we first began. They, particularly the girls, are becoming more confident and self-assured every year.

Too Many Cellphones

The bridge we financed is done!! Tangi Saidan, a village outside Kabul, just completed the footbridge over a section of river that for several months of the year could not be crossed—or not crossed without sacrificing the dignity lost every time a woman raised her dress or skirt to avoid getting wet. In Afghanistan anything above the ankle is considered risqué. Afghan men are woefully repressed and, if anything, need to see more leg not less. How else will they be able to "get over it?"

The new bridge saves a one-mile walk and eliminates "indecent" crossings for over ten thousand people. In honor and recognition of the achievement, we planned to visit Tangi Saidan, spend time with villagers, and walk across the bridge.

Wasay, a leader in Tangi Saidan, advised us against coming even though villagers would welcome the opportunity to meet and thank us personally. "You will be safe from your hotel to Tangi Saidan," he said, "and you will be safe while you are with us; but there are too many cellphones in this country, and someone who sees you here could call to arrange your kidnapping on your return to Kabul." I will cross that bridge someday, but, not this trip.

Saving Girls from Aging Out

We met with Nazar, the programs director for Ashiana, an Afghan non-profit organization providing educational and humanitarian programs that benefit working street children. Nazar told us about a Provincial Reconstruction Team (PRT) that had been financing an Ashiana program the past two years in Parwan.

PRT's are the "good guys" with money to spend on reconstruction projects and programs. Each operates in its own designated area and, as fate would have it, the PRT funding this program had recently been assigned to another region. It could no longer finance the program.

Ashiana has been unable to obtain contact information for the PRT currently assigned to Parwan. Contact lists for government and private aid organizations have proven impossible to locate. If there are lists, they are not being shared.

The three-year program began two years ago when one hundred and twenty Afghan girls entered into an accelerated education curriculum with the understanding that, if they completed and passed all courses, they would be admitted to high school.

These students were too old to attend school at their proficiency level, having "aged out." If by Spring 2011 they are not ready to enter high school, they will be "aged out" permanently. If the program is not reinstated, the formal education of one hundred and twenty girls will end abruptly and forever.

The budget for twelve months is twenty-eight thousand dollars, less than twenty dollars per month per child. Once again we are confronted with how little it takes to alter lives. Before leaving Kabul we agreed to fund this project and reopen the doors. It costs less than two thousand five hundred dollars a month. We'll find a way to raise the money. It's just too important not to.

CHAPTER 9

Events in 2010
When to Give.

❖   ❖   ❖

THE REPORTS OF INJURIES, DEATHS, violence, corruption, destruction, and desperate conditions in Haiti following its 7.0 earthquake in January portray conditions I have observed in Afghanistan since my first visit in 2005. Haiti is the fourth poorest country in the world and Afghanistan is the fifth. No one I've met appreciates how dire conditions are in Afghanistan except Afghans. It is amazing how many have responded to the call for aid to Haiti through their cellphone! Alexander Graham Bell's "electrical speech machine", invented in 1876, has become a powerful fundraising device, an outcome not likely to have been foreseen.

When natural disasters occur, wait before contributing. In time you will be able to identify individuals and organizations on the ground worthy of your support. Once the news cameras move on, donations drop dramatically. Emergency relief is important. Equally important, if not more, are reconstruction dollars. Temporary relief is just that—temporary. Meaningful change is achieved over time. Haiti, like Afghanistan, will need reconstruction aid for years.

Fundraising by the way is like panning for gold. You sift through a lot of sand before discovering a nugget. The most valuable nuggets of all are donors that recognize the need to provide support over time. There is no quick fix to educating a child.

WHY DIDN'T I THINK OF THAT?

In February, I attended a dinner in Sausalito held by the National Defense University (NDU). Every year, over sixty countries send one or two of their top military leaders to NDU in Washington, DC. Bringing military leaders together for almost a year is an ingenious program. Friendships, including among adversaries, are formed as they work, play, and study together. They also travel extensively throughout the United States, meeting with Americans, discovering how large and diverse our country is.

I was seated with Mohammad Sultani, an Afghan Brigadier General, and six other military leaders from other countries. The evening included a discussion of Pakistan and how important it is to Afghanistan's future that the Taliban not be given safe havens inside Pakistan. "Will the Pakistan Army defeat the Taliban?" I asked. The first and only response was "No, the United States is paying Pakistan to fight the Taliban. If they defeat the Taliban, you will no longer pay them to fight them." No one had given me this analysis before and it is one I had never considered. It makes perfect sense to workers building a bridge to never finish.

When asked about TIE's work in Afghanistan, I couldn't resist the temptation to tell them about our experience with microcredit loans—namely that the success rate for microcredit loans made to men is abysmal. Loans to women, on the other hand, have a payback rate of over 95%. The men at our table weren't surprised to learn women are more credit-worthy than men.

Other topics discussed and opinions solicited that night included, "Should women be in the military?" "Not on the front line." "Should gays?" "No." What have you observed while in the United States?" "Americans are very friendly." "You elect your government. That is very important." "I didn't realize how large the United States is." "There is more tolerance in the United States for people who are different." The food was excellent, the view from Sausalito to San Francisco extraordinary, and while

these professional warriors laughed and joked with one another over dinner, I wondered, why is world peace so difficult to achieve?

A Great Start
The fundraising event for the girls' school to be built in Farza was
held on March 25th. Susan Paulson, Alan Hyman, the Americans for
Philanthropy, Khaled Hosseini, Ambassador Tayeb Jawad, our keynote
speaker, and inspired donors, made it possible for Nabi and I to personally deliver this message to villagers in Farza two weeks later: "Bring
us your construction plans". We raised sixty-eight thousand dollars that
night.

What are They Thinking?
Nabi and I arrived in Kabul last Friday shortly after President Karzai publicly announced he might "join the Taliban." As if we don't have enough
problems raising funds, not to mention the increased security risk his
statement will create for us. President Karzai is reacting to recent criti-
cisms publicly lodged against him by our government. He is also responding to accusations by the Taliban that he is an American "puppet." These
public pronouncements by our government and President Karzai make
absolutely no sense.

Undermining public support for President Karzai plays into the hands
of the Taliban. It is exactly what they are attempting to achieve. On the
other hand, President Karzai, in aligning himself with the Taliban, is
jeopardizing his request for financial support from the United States and
others.

The Afghan government does not have the funds necessary to maintain an army and police force large enough to defeat the Taliban. Everyone
knows that. Whatever disagreements exist between us and President

Karzai should remain behind closed doors. Everyone loses when disagreements go public, except the Taliban.

PRIVACY RIGHTS

Our effort to provide a soccer field in Tangi Saidan has come to a halt. We had reached a lease agreement with a farmer and were days away from providing money to level the land and install goalposts. What happened? Kuchi nomads, who for years have been camping and grazing their sheep near the site, set up camp. They insisted that the field not be built.

Why not? Because boys and mature men would be able to look from the soccer field into their camp. The women and older girls living there would be forced to stay inside their tents during practices and while games were being played. Custom and security concerns require many Afghan women to remain out of sight.

The tribe's right to privacy could have been challenged by going ahead. It's not their land. We were, however, told the tribe would enforce its perceived "right to privacy." In Afghanistan, self-help is, unfortunately, more often than not the first resort and not the last. There is no effective, reliable, and corruption-free judicial system in most areas of Afghanistan. Going to court is the last resort.

We had been informed of a killing that occurred nearby because someone had refused to stop his children and their friends from playing volleyball. They were "making too much noise." No one, including us, was willing to find out what the Kuchi tribe would do if we went ahead. The search for another location has begun.

THE HORSE WON'T DRINK

Nineteen village *maliks* (leaders) in the Char Asiab valley are preparing a list of two hundred of their poorest farmers. Over the past couple of years, we've helped farmers in that area by sharing the cost of vegetable seeds and fertilizer. Nabi sells grain seeds around the world and we are able to buy and deliver seeds at his vendors' wholesale cost. We knew the quality of the seeds would be superior to what the farmers were able to buy.

Seeds were provided for free the first and second year, enabling everyone to test their quality and production. We split the cost of fertilizer. The combination increased their yields by a factor of three to four times normal: proof of concept done.

This year we proposed to split the cost of the seeds and fertilizer, but they will not agree to share in the cost of seeds. Our goal in providing financial assistance is to build programs that become self-supporting. These are the only programs that last.

Knowing that a self-sustaining program cannot be established, it is time to move on. This year we will share the cost of fertilizer and not send seeds. Next year they are on their own. We will revisit this again when they understand we are not interested in establishing programs that must be subsidized forever or when my lottery numbers hit.

A TIME TO UPGRADE

We visited a computer course funded by TIE and overseen by Ashiana, an Afghan NGO that helps educate and support street children. The course is taught by Mehrab Karimi. He loves his job, having worked on the streets himself as a child.

The law firm of Farella, Braun, and Martel donated over 100 computers when they upgraded their own, thus making it possible for us to support several computer classes. Afghan schools have computer classes. Almost all do not have computers. Your computer is probably running slow and doesn't have enough storage capacity. Give us your antiquated machine. They can use whatever we don't.

What it Takes to Matriculate

In Parwan, we visited the accelerated educational program for girls that we rescued when it lost funding last year. There are 120 girls in the program and to catch up with children their own age, they must learn in one year what is normally taught in two. That means no winter break and starting classes at 6:30 in the morning instead of 8 a.m. At noon they eat lunch at school. In the afternoon they can attend sewing or beauty school classes. Tutoring is also available in the afternoon for girls having trouble with any of the subjects taught. A year from now those who pass a national exam will be integrated into the school system. Those who fail will have "aged out." These are by far the most accomplished and dedicated students we've met.

Importing Handmade Products

Parwan students asked whether we could sell items they made in the United States. This is a question I'm often asked. Most want to produce clothing, embroidered items or carpets that are very labor-intensive products to produce. Even if we could eliminate and become the "middleman," it's extremely difficult to pay much for labor and be competitive with products made in other countries. Afghan tailors, in fact, find it difficult to make and sell clothes in Afghanistan because they must compete with clothing made in China. As long as labor is cheap in competing countries, Afghan workers will never get what we or they would consider fair compensation for their labor.

If we became their "middleman," we'd become "the man," the one who makes most of the money. This could easily destroy the goodwill we've earned over the last several years.

Breaking the Deadlock

When we landed in Kabul in October, Basir handed us a contract proposal drafted by the Ministry of Education. It governed the construction of the school for girls in Farza for which the architectural plans had been bouncing around the construction department for weeks with no end in sight. A permit to build would not be issued until we signed the contract but this one was unacceptable. The fundamental problem being that it made TIE responsible for the school's construction.

We had explained to the villagers from the very beginning that the school was theirs, not ours. They would need to obtain whatever approvals were required and accept responsibility for design and construction, while TIE would provide the materials, in accordance with an agreed upon budget. We knew immediately that we must meet with someone higher on the organization chart.

That evening at the hotel while I was enjoying a chocolate fix with a Tylenol chaser, Nabi was having dinner with a friend who could arrange a meeting with the Minister of Education, Farooq Wardak. Sixteen hours later, Minister Wardak signed a Memorandum of Understanding consistent with our agreement that I had prepared in advance of our meeting. He also "made a call." After the call he said, "They need to understand we need your help and they should do everything they can to help you." The school for girls in Farza instantly became a fast track project within the building department.

A Rough Beginning

To celebrate, we suggested they have a ribbon-cutting ceremony Thursday or Friday morning, letting them know we were returning home Friday. We were advised that a number of officials would not be able to attend on either day and suggested we change our return travel plans to next week. There is one day Nabi and I will never change and that is the day we're scheduled to leave.

Life is just too difficult, confining, troubling and dangerous in Afghanistan to stay longer than we must. From the moment we arrive until we board the plane home, we're counting down the days and hours. Moreover, the longer we stay the greater the risk that we will be harmed. Unlike cats, we have only one life.

Last night, we were told by Ehsan, Farza's project manager, that the only day that would work would be the following day. We purposely told him we would arrive at 2 p.m. to avoid anyone having to prepare lunch. In Afghanistan, it is understood that if guests are present during a meal, they must be fed. Not only must a guest be fed, it can be taken as an insult to not accept an invitation. Our 2 p.m. arrival strategy failed. Peer pressure forced Ehsan to prepare a feast and we agreed to arrive by 1 p.m. Ehsan held nothing back. It was the best and largest meal I'd ever had since coming to Afghanistan.

At the ceremony, the Governor of Farza spoke first then I followed. I told those present that we share the love of children, know how important education is to their future, and how happy we were to be able to contribute to the construction of the school. I ended by affirming that today was just the beginning of what would be a long-term relationship.

I had no idea what the governor said until informed by Nabi during our ride back to Kabul. He complained about the short notice and lack of preparation for the ceremony, noting there was no stage or musicians. He said the villagers would not find enough volunteers to build the school and we would need to pay the workers. Essentially he said "thank you for your support, it's not enough, the plan won't work, and this is an ill-planned, cheap ribbon-cutting ceremony." Absent from his speech was a call for volunteers to build the school.

Celebrate good times? Not quite.

Nabi, fortunately, allowed me to remain oblivious to what the governor said until I was out of earshot. I would have responded in kind and later realized there was no need. A politician who bets against his followers needn't be challenged by an outsider. He did more damage to himself than I could. I look forward to the day the school opens.

The lunch took so long that the headmaster let the girls, who were waiting for the ceremony to begin, go home. While driving back to Kabul, I thought about the day. Ehsan prepared a feast, a burden we sought to avoid. The only person who spoke other than me, predicted we would fail. Not a single girl or woman was present to celebrate the commencement of construction of a school for girls. It could have been worse. We could have delayed our return trip home and had the same experience the following week.

When Trust is in Short Supply

Trust, or the lack thereof, is a major problem in Afghanistan. Everyone suspects everyone else of being on the take. It's hard to believe otherwise when *baksheesh*, (a gift), is routinely given to or demanded by officials providing services for which they are already being paid. It's one of the "cultural differences" we try to ignore. If called upon, we needed to be able to prove what we spent on materials. A purchasing process was agreed upon.

First, the villager's engineer provided a list of materials that would last for two weeks. He and the villagers then designated the suppliers they recommended and the prices they were quoted. Basir had the ability to shop for better prices and recommend other vendors. Once vendors and prices were agreed upon, materials were purchased with Basir and Ehsan present along with anyone else the villagers wanted to include.

Ehsan and Basir were each given a receipt signed by the vendor and themselves. That way both would be able to prove what was purchased and how much was paid. Before another purchase was made, Basir visited the job site. He would verify the need for additional materials and send us photos of the progress made.

It was a cumbersome and imperfect system, I admit. People could always accuse or suspect Basir, Ehsan, and the others involved of sharing kickbacks and falsifying receipts. A perfect checks and balance system is impossible to devise in a country where corruption is common and trust is rarely given.

Bucket Brigade—Literally

Today one hundred and twenty-two buckets of fortified rice, donated by Stop Hunger Now, were distributed to students from the poorest families chosen by teachers working for TIE. The rice was in buckets to keep out rats and mice during transit. Tomorrow the rice along with clothing will be distributed to Ashiana's entire school—two hundred and eighty students in all. Seventy-eight of them are sponsored by TIE's supporters.

The balance of the rice and clothing will be distributed to IDPs (internally displaced persons) living in camps in Kabul. That's fifteen thousand pounds of clothing, blankets, shoes, school supplies, and toys that people no longer needed and brought to a packing party. We may argue about redistribution of wealth. There should be little or no debate about the need to redistribute our stuff. Set yours aside, and bring it to our next packing party.

A Land Mine Victim

Two days ago we met Gul Waro, one of Farzana's students. She's twenty-six years old and lost both legs to a land mine. On her way to meet with us, her wheelchair tipped over twice, spilling her onto the road. Nabi went to Kabul the next day and bought her a sturdy replacement. She won't be spilled onto the street again.

The chair was wheeled in as a surprise. She was sitting in a desk at the back of the room where we could not wheel it to her and, seeing this, she lowered herself to the floor and crawled to where she could be lifted in. This was the first time I had seen anyone crawl without legs. She cried, and Nabi and I came very close to joining her. We have added her to our sponsorship list, and she will receive monthly financial support from this day forward. This is one of many incidents we've experienced that simultaneously brought both sorrow and joy into our lives.

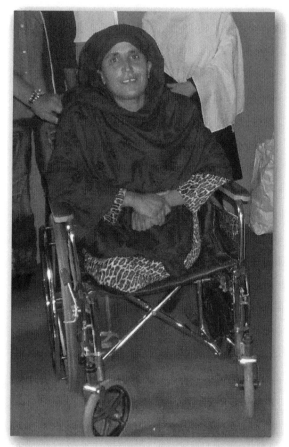
Gul, a landmine victim with her new chair.

TAKING RESPONSIBILITY FOR ONE LIFE

Ashiana, a nonprofit organization located in Kabul, established a sponsorship program that enables sponsors to provide financial support to individual street children. We followed their lead and started a sponsorship program this year, run by Qudsia, Basir's wife and Suzanne Rogge, a volunteer without whom this program would not be possible. Together they now have seventy Afghan children to care for.

Street children work on the streets of Kabul washing cars, selling gum, collecting paper, begging, shining shoes, and doing whatever generates income. Most cannot attend school because their families need the money they make. The streets are dangerous, rob children of their childhoods, and make it extremely difficult for them to keep up with their peers.

He would rather be in school.

Sponsored children and their parents or guardians must sign written agreements obligating them to go to school and get off the streets. In exchange, they receive a monthly stipend. If a child is found working after sponsorship begins, they will lose their sponsorship. We must have a firm "off the streets policy," otherwise the temptation to keep children working would be too great.

When we first began, we were told that twenty dollars a month would be enough. We then enlisted over twenty-five sponsors at that rate. Six months later when Nabi and I met with the children, several admitted they were still working. Twenty dollars a month was, in fact, not enough. Many were earning more than that on the streets, and their families could not afford to absorb the difference.

Basir and Qudsia determined that forty dollars would be a reasonable amount. When I returned to the United States, I undertook the unpleasant task of writing sponsors, informing them of the problem and asking them to double their support. All but one agreed. It was reassuring to know that we are trusted.

A few years after the program began, several of the sponsors had decided to increase their support from forty to fifty dollars a month so that, come payday, some children walked away with fifty dollars and others with forty. This, in turn, led to children asking for more in their letters to their sponsor. They reasonably assumed that those receiving fifty dollars had asked for it, but the increases had occurred solely because sponsors had wanted to provide additional support to "their kids."

The children have been told to not ask for money or things in their letters to their sponsor. Requests for additional support must now be submitted through Qudsia and Basir who have the right to say no or pass the request on to us. We in turn decide whether to forward their request to their sponsor. Requests that survive this filtering process are generally granted, particularly for tutoring and additional classes. TIE generally picks up the tab for additional courses when sponsors reach their limit. Courses taught outside the schools cost between ten and twenty dollars a month, a small contribution to make toward a motivated child's education.

Over time, we have been able to increase monthly support to fifty dollars for every sponsored child. We prefer to keep the support levels as close as possible to minimize the luck-of-the-draw impact on support.

The additional ten dollars a month has had a major impact on families. Most apply the extra money toward the education of their child.

I have watched commercials claiming that a child can be supported for twenty-five dollars a month. I believe this amount was established by marketing gurus who based their decision on what they thought the donor market would bear. Twenty-five dollars a month is not enough to meet basic needs.

If you are able to establish a direct connection with a child and his or her family, err on the high side. The goal is not to move the needle from abject poverty to subsistence living. We know from years of experience that fifty dollars a month will, for most families in Afghanistan, cover a child's cost to attend school and put some food on the table. When supporting families struggling on the bottom of the economic ladder, the goal should be to move them up at least one rung. The likelihood of them being able to move higher on their own will be greatly improved.

One added benefit of providing fifty dollars a month is that it's enough to justify incurring the expense of a girl's education. There are families in TIE's sponsorship program where the only daughter going to school is the one sponsored through TIE. As small as the cost of this is, some parents keep their daughters home because they "can't afford to allow her to go."

An Afghan girl who brings home fifty dollars a month will likely be a significant contributor to her family's income. We cannot force families to allow their daughters to go to school, but we can eliminate the economic barrier to going.

I SHOULD HAVE KNOWN

Zohra and Nelab were our first sponsored students to graduate from high school and now they want financial assistance to go to college. Nabi and I met with both girls and their mothers. I wanted to reach an agreement that if I were able to raise the thousand dollars a year needed for college, their daughters would be allowed to complete their college education and go as far as they could. I was concerned that a forced marriage might bring an end to their studies.

Married Afghan women don't go to school. We have had two sponsored young girls forced to drop out of school when they were forced to marry. One was fourteen years old. I thought it was important to be Zohra's and Nelab's advocate, knowing full well that their mothers' promise would not be enforceable.

As Nabi explained my concern, Zohra's mother turned to me with an all-knowing smile and said, "Tell Budd not to worry. I don't want Zohra to turn out like me. I was forced to marry at fourteen. My daughter's life will be better than mine."

Street children are highly motivated. They know how important education is to their future. We've only had a few leave the program. In addition to the marriage dropout, three children moved away from Kabul; one fell ill, couldn't afford health care, and died; and three were dropped from the program because, in their mother's words, "they were lazy" and "not doing their work." The "lazy" students had been given several chances, were placed on probation, and ultimately proved to us that their mothers were right.

SKYPE BRIDGES THE GAP

Several schools in the United States are supporting street children with the funds they raise, and I report to them annually on the progress of the children they sponsor. We were able to arrange a Skype encounter between Corte Madera students in Los Gatos and the four Afghan children they had been supporting for years. The electronic transmission was anything but perfect, however the impact on the young people in both worlds was powerful.

The sponsorship program is Nabi's and my favorite. We've watched Afghan children who are dirty, poorly-dressed, malnourished, insecure, afraid, and shy transition into just the opposite. As trite as it may seem, we've seen the power of hope when injected into the lives of those who had little. The program also enables American boys and girls to contrast their lives with those of children they are supporting, and it affords them the opportunity to experience the joy of directly making a difference. It accomplishes what every parent attempts to instill in their children.

SPELLING BEES

We held two spelling contests this year, one in the spring and the other in the fall. In the spring, there were two groups: fourth and fifth graders; sixth and seventh graders. In the fall, we added a third group: eighth and ninth graders. Teachers working for TIE were asked to select two of their best students for each group. There were at least twenty competitors per group, all excited as they had never held a spelling contest before.

We provided one bus to transport the competitors. Worried that families might not allow their daughters to ride with boys, we were willing to provide two if necessary. They arrived in one—boys seated on one side, girls on the other. There is very little interaction between boys and girls either inside or outside the classroom.

The contest was held in the learning center built by Wahid on his property with several of his friends. The center is essentially a large room with desks, a chalkboard at one end, bookcases, a rug, and a few light bulbs dangling from the ceiling. Electricity is provided by a loud, unreliable generator that chooses when it wants to work. Wrought-iron bars shield small, dirty windows that do not allow enough sunlight in. The room reeks of clay, old straw, and tired lumber, materials used in its construction. The classroom lacks almost everything except enthusiasm. In the words of Khalid Hosseini, "Afghan children have an insatiable appetite for education."

We gave the teachers authority to select and buy over five hundred books and designated Wahid as its librarian. He proudly showed me his record keeping. Given how little time he is called upon as a librarian, Wahid, on an hourly basis, is the highest-paid employee we have, receiving one-hundred twenty-five dollars a month. Of course he, like everyone else, asks for a raise every time we visit.

Wahid's wife, Zeba, teaches Dari in the center six days a week, three hours a day, for $150 per month. She has been the breadwinner in their family. Wahid, whose greatest assets are his energy and enthusiasm for helping children, has been otherwise unemployed for ten years. He has never refused to do anything we've asked and willingly takes on more responsibility.

Farzana, one of TIE's most vocal and insistent teachers, selected the words that our contestants would be asked to spell. Each was written on a small piece of paper that was folded and put in one of two piles: easy and difficult. Competitors were given two chips. If they misspelled a word, they turned in a chip. When they turned in their second, they were out.

When a contestant's name was called, he or she would pick one of the folded pieces of paper and hand it to Farzana. The student then went to the chalkboard to write the word she called out. They were allowed to make changes. When satisfied with their spelling, they'd turn and face Farzan who was the judge.

Almost every student present competed. Nabi and I had to keep reminding them that they were not allowed to help one another. Students would shout out a letter when a competitor was stuck and groan when they wrote down a letter that was wrong. Friends wanted friends to succeed, even if it jeopardized their own chance of winning. Competitors helping each other succeed was a phenomenon I hadn't seen or ever experienced myself. It came naturally to them. Our "no-help-from-the-audience" rule was ignored several times—They didn't think the rule was fair or reasonable!

The improvement in their spelling between the first and second contests was remarkable. In the fall, Farzana stopped letting contestants pull words from the easy pile. After two rounds, no one had made a mistake. The second group took two hours to narrow the field to two finalists. Both were girls, and neither had lost a chip.

The two finalists stood by the chalkboard as Farzana pulled words from the difficult pile. Fifteen minutes later, neither had made a mistake, and the pile was gone. Farzana called out words to spell until she couldn't think of any more. Then members of the audience began to shout out words, and Farzana decided which would be used in the contest. Ten minutes later, everyone was quiet. The audience had given up. Nabi took over and spent ten more minutes trying to stump the girls.

At a loss for words, literally, Nabi shouted above the laughter, "Spell Intercontinental." The entire room erupted, laughing and shouting at Nabi, objecting to the request to spell a word in English. The contestants didn't object. The loser failed by only one letter and graciously accepted her defeat.

Every contestant received a backpack donated by Kelly Grimmer, one of TIE's supporters. The top three spellers in each group were awarded cash prizes: thirty dollars for first place, twenty for second, and ten for third. Afghan laborers were making eight dollars a day. The first-place winner was likely the breadwinner in her family that week and may have been for the month.

The spelling bees are very popular with the children, teachers, and parents. They provide an opportunity for boys and girls to travel by bus together and compete against one another in the same room. Girls outperformed the boys, which is an accomplishment that supports the case for gender equality.

The spelling contests are risky events. They bring boys and girls together at a function sponsored by an American organization that advocates and supports the education of girls. They could be targeted, particularly if it is known we will be present.

Our purpose in holding the contests was to demonstrate how motivational and fun they can be, and how easy they are to organize. They can hold spelling bees without us and we'd be happy to pay for the bus and prizes. Our role is to serve as a catalyst for change, step aside when we can, and continue to provide financial support where needed.

CHAPTER 10

Events in 2011
Porch Privileges

❖ ❖ ❖

ANYONE WHO RECEIVES NEWSLETTERS FROM us has porch privileges. Porch privileges entitle them to drop their stuff on my porch knowing that someday it will reach an Afghan family living seven thousand, three hundred and ninety-four miles away in a tent or mud hut, or a family chosen by our teachers as among the poorest of the poor. Porch privileges are not without rules and regulations:

1. If it takes two people to lift a box or bag, it's too heavy. Jack and I load everything that's left on my porch and we're on Medicare. Neither want to reach the "donut hole."
2. No underwear or high heeled shoes. Yes, we've received both.
3. Porch privileges can't be shared and are non-transferable. Jack and I can't handle more than a couple of tons without ending up stooped over, leaning against walls or flat on our backs.
4. Don't stack higher than the porch railing. Some think it's unsightly however, I think it's beautiful, knowing what impact it will have when distributed.

WOMEN'S RIGHTS AND PET ROCKS

We've been helping Afghan children and families for more than eight years. Progress is painfully slow particularly in impacting rights for women. In the interests of maintaining peace and in furtherance of our country's exit strategy, there is evidence to suggest women's rights may "take a back seat" to other priorities.

The following quote is taken from an article in the *The Washington Post,* by Rajiv Chandrasekaran: "Gender issues are going to have to take a back seat to other priorities," said a senior United States official involved in Afghan policy, who spoke on the condition of anonymity, to discuss internal policy deliberations. "There is no way we can be successful if we maintain every special interest and pet project. All those pet rocks in our rucksack were taking us down." [3]

Gender issues are "pet rocks in our rucksack that were taking us down?" "Were" as in past tense? Has a policy decision been made to unload gender issues from the rucksack?

Gender issues weigh heavily on Afghan women and girls every day of their lives. They are living in a country rated by the United Nations as among the worst countries in the world for a woman to be born. Has advancing women's rights become so burdensome that they must be dropped from the agenda? Human rights including women's should never be given a back seat or cast aside. This comment was surely made by a man.

APRIL REPORT FROM KABUL
YET ANOTHER BUREAUCRATIC HURDLE

Nabi and I arrived in Kabul on Friday. Our trips almost always involve solving bureaucratic problems that Basir has not been able to resolve on his own. Nabi is, through the many friends he has in Kabul, able to arrange meetings with people higher on the organizational charts of government ministries. The unresolved problem addressed today is obtaining approval for another shipment of fortified rice donated by Stop Hunger Now (forty-four thousand packages or two hundred sixty-four thousand meals). We have received approval for and successfully distributed a shipment of their rice before. Why then should there be a problem now?

A man inside the Ministry of Health has decided there should be an expiration date on each package of rice. According to him, they "had made a mistake" allowing the prior shipments. We explained to him that Stop Hunger Now has distributed over forty million packages of rice to seventy-six different countries. No other country requires an expiration date on each package. The rice is purchased within a few months of packaging and has a shelf life of three years. The rice is consumed within a month or two after we distribute it. Essentially he is requiring expiration dates on rice with a three-year shelf life that's given to people who are starving. What, a package of rice may get lost in the pantry and spoil!?

The rice packages are packed at packing parties. Volunteers weigh each portion, add nutrients, put the ingredients in a package and seal it. We then pack the packages of rice into five-gallon plastic buckets to prevent any rat invasions in transit.

The only way to date each package would be to stamp a date on each one or apply labels by hand. I contacted Rick Kearney from Stop Hunger Now, expecting him to say, "It's impossible." He didn't. His exact words were, "Tell me what they want…bring it on." I was, but shouldn't have been, surprised by Rick's response. The humanitarian aid world attracts the most caring and passionate among us.

Fortunately, Nabi, through a friend, arranged a meeting with the chief of staff to the Minister of Health. We explained the problem and he met briefly with the Minister. Five minutes later he returned, made "the call," and told us to meet again with the man who was blocking the shipment. "If this is not resolved, come back," he said. The Minister of Health, by the way, is a woman!

Dating of each package was no longer necessary, but now he insisted the rice be tested by their lab. I had brought some rice packages with me.

The truth is, the rice we wanted to ship would not be the same as the rice we gave them. Had I disclosed this fact, he would have required us to get them a sample of that.

There is no mail delivery to Afghanistan, and if we used DHL, Afghanistan's customs office would become involved. It's possible the customs office would not have allowed the rice to come into the country. At a minimum this process would take several months.

When Afghan government officials impose onerous and unreasonable requirements, there is always the possibility that they want a bribe. It is impossible to know whether they expect a bribe, unless they ask. He didn't and neither did we. So, the samples have gone off to be tested, a useless waste of their time and money. Had Nabi not known someone who could arrange a meeting with the Minister of Health, two hundred sixty-four thousand meals would never had made it to families living in the camps.

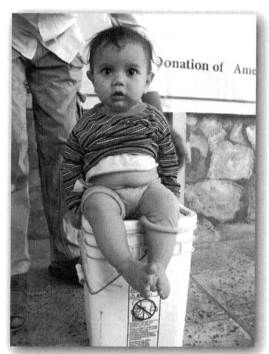

Squatter's Rights! He's claiming his bucket of rice.

On To the Minister of Education

Having resolved the impasse created by the Ministry of Health, we then proceeded to address a problem created by the Ministry of Education. It had decided that the villagers in Farza would need to apply for a new building permit. Why? Because the "work stopped," and a new permit was therefore required. The work didn't stop. The men didn't work during the winter because it was too cold. They took a winter break. The new permit requirement triggered a struggle for control over the project. Whoever gains control is in a position to receive a bribe which, of course, we are unwilling to give.

Ehsan and Basir are the designated project managers under the existing building permit. Ehsan showed us a letter from the local branch of the Ministry of Education applying for a new permit wherein another man would be appointed as manager of the project. Neither us, nor anyone else, had been consulted about this designation. Upon learning of this takeover attempt, several villagers met. They were ready to march on the powers that be and call a meeting of the *Shura* (local council) to contest the usurpation of control. Nabi's advice was, "Get the permit, start construction and struggle over who's in charge after the permit is issued." Sound advice, once again.

The following day Ehsan went to the building department with the letter in hand to apply for a new permit, fully expecting them to appoint their replacement as the project manager. The building department refused, stating, "What qualifications does he have to run a construction project?" They then appointed the village's engineer instead and gave Ehsan a new permit. Having the village's engineer as project manager is fine with us. He is "their guy" and has the expertise necessary to work with the building department.

We don't yet know if the takeover conspirators know their designee wasn't appointed. All we know is tensions are so high in the village that we've been advised to not visit the jobsite this trip. The bottom line in all this jockeying for power is that we still and always will hold the trump card. The money to finish building the school is held in our U.S. bank account and will only be released when conditions are right. Gifts and bribes are not in the budget and never will be.

Meeting with "Our" Sponsored Children

The good news and most rewarding part of the trip occurred today when we met with seventy-six street children sponsored through TIE. They are extraordinary considering the life they've led and how hard they must work to catch up with students their age. We have several sponsored children who rank in the top ten of their class and several whose national test scores are improving. Many of the classes have 50 students or more. Tomorrow we award prizes to the winners of a writing contest we sponsored. If we could only spend all of our time with the children! In my next life, I'd definitely like to come back as a teacher but not in Afghanistan for all the reasons that are obvious.

Too Poor to Marry

On the assumption you don't drink your morning coffee while reading the Kabul-E-News, I decided to pass along an article they recently published on April 7, written by Usman Shariff. If you've paid for a wedding, you'll identify:

"As a civil servant Afghan Ahmad Mahfouz earns nearly ten times the average salary in his impoverished homeland, but he still cannot afford to marry his fiancée. Already thousands of dollars in debt after hosting a lavish engagement party for 500 guests in December, Mahfouz says he doesn't know how he will ever afford the kind of wedding his wife to be and her family expect. Expensive weddings have become a barrier to marriages, and the Afghan government may step in.

"I owe money to almost everyone I know, and I have no idea how I will ever earn enough to get married," said the twenty-seven-year-old, one of a growing number of middle-class Afghans struggling with the escalating cost of weddings. Since the fall of the Taliban nearly a decade ago, marriage ceremonies in Afghan cities have gone from being simple family affairs to lavish parties for up to one thousand family and friends in specially built wedding halls. The ability to put on such an ostentatious display of wealth has become a test of honor for the groom, who tradition- ally foots the entire bill himself and sometimes also has to pay a dowry to his bride's family.

Concerned that the high cost of weddings is forcing young people to delay marriage, the Afghan government is considering banning extrava- gant weddings, which experts say are often the result of competition be- tween newly rich clans. A new bill being proposed by the justice ministry would restrict the number of guests at a wedding party to three hundred and limit spending per guest to two hundred fifty Afghanis (about five dollars). Sociologist Barayalai Fetrat said, "The extravagant ceremonies were a new and predominantly urban phenomenon in Afghanistan, which has seen a massive influx of foreign money in recent years in the form of aid and military spending. The billions of dollars that have flooded into Afghanistan have made some people very rich and those people have come up with new ways to display their wealth. Expensive weddings have no root in our culture," he added, bemoaning the high social costs of the new trend in a country where the average annual income is five hundred forty dollars[4]."

Note: The Afghan government has not imposed a limitation on what can be spent. The absurdity of what is becoming a social more was, however, openly discussed. Whatever happened to the weddings held by the river in a public park with a few close friends, some of whom were happy to bring potato salad or coleslaw. By the way, whatever happened to grape Jello embedded with canned fruit cocktail and marshmallows? After all, spam has survived the passage of time.

DOOR TO DOOR SELLING EDUCATION

We met with Farzana today and she spent a considerable amount of time discussing how she convinces families to allow their daughters to attend her classes. She makes house calls accompanied by her mother. When not successful in convincing parents, she enlists their family, friends, and neighbors to help change their minds. She corners parents at funerals, engagement parties and weddings. She's relentless.

Farzana proudly informed us that there are over 100 girls now in school whose education started in her home. She's been working for TIE for three years. When asked why parents, particularly fathers, do not allow their daughters to go to school, she said, "They are not educated. They do not see the value of an education. Girls become wives and mothers. They don't think it's important for girls to be educated. Boys are expected to make money and it's important that they be educated." I asked whether religion played a role in denying girls access to an education. "No, they just don't see the value," she responded.

DO YOU SPEAK ENGLISH?

Nabi and I are headed home tomorrow. We will be adding more before and after school classes in math, science, English, and computers. It's very difficult to find English teachers, particularly outside the city limits of Kabul. Yesterday we learned how important it is to interview prospective English teachers before they're hired. Our interview with a candidate recommended to us by the principal of a school where he would teach went as follows:

Me: "Thank you for coming. Let's you and I just talk awhile in English, OK?"
Candidate: (*Silence*).
Me: "Do you speak English?"

Candidate: "No, I don't understand."
Nabi (in Dari): "How can you teach English if you cannot carry on a conversation in English?"
Candidate in Dari: "I can teach them words. They are not educated in our village. It will be OK."

The candidate the school principal proposed can't speak or understand English! He had to learn English and stay at least one lesson ahead of his students. This school is located less than a forty-five-minute drive from Kabul, an indication of how difficult it is to find qualified teachers outside the capital.

Going out into the "underserved areas" sounds good until you realize these areas don't have enough qualified teachers, particularly female teachers. If a village doesn't allow girls to be taught by a male teacher and it doesn't have a qualified female teacher in the village or find one willing to commute, there is little that can be done to educate girls in that village. The underserved areas are underserved for reasons other than being neglected or overlooked. The brain drain that occurred during the Russian occupation, the civil wars that followed and the reign of the Taliban was substantial.

THE GREAT DIVIDE
One challenge we face is to inform and enlist others to support the reconstruction effort underway in Afghanistan. The merits, or lack thereof, of wars we've financed or waged have been argued *ad nauseam*. Whatever side anyone is on, the consequences of war are there for everyone to see. It's easy to be anti-war, but we must also be pro-victim and proactive in helping victims rebuild their lives. Therein lies the great divide—those who know and "do" and those who know and "don't."

Mother's Index

Kathy Vizas, a TIE volunteer, sent me an article, "The 2011 Mother's Index," which summarizes the results of Save the Children's twelfth annual Mother's Index. The index compares the well-being of mothers and children in 164 countries. How did Afghanistan do? It finished in last place. They concluded Afghanistan "is the worst place in the world for a mother to be." A few statistics relating to Afghanistan taken from the report are:

1. One child in five does not reach his or her fifth birthday. At this rate, every mother is likely to suffer the loss of a child.
2. One woman in eleven dies in pregnancy or childbirth.
3. The average woman does not see her forty-fifth birthday.
4. Women earn twenty-five cents or less for every dollar men earn.
5. A typical female receives fewer than five years of formal education.
6. One child in three suffers from malnutrition.

The author wrote, "Statistics are far more than numbers. It is the human despair and lost opportunities behind these numbers that call for changes to ensure that mothers everywhere have the basic tools they need to break the cycle of poverty and improve the quality of life for themselves, their children, and for generations to come." [5]

It's only a few days until Mother's Day, which makes these statistics for Afghan mothers even more troubling. On the other hand, they afford us an opportunity to appreciate what we have, celebrate what we've been able to accomplish together, and affirm our commitment to do more.

Surviving in the worst place in the world for a mother to be.

THE RICE WAS APPROVED!

The Ministry of Health approved the shipment of forty-four thousand packages of rice yesterday. They will be on their way to Afghanistan soon. "Soon" is a relative concept, and I'm struggling to become more patient. As a nation we're too "stressed out" and would benefit from a slower paced lifestyle.

BURGLARY AND FALL OUT

The learning center located on Wahid's property was burglarized and computers were stolen. Thanks to the San Francisco law firm of Farella,

Braun, and Martel, we have enough to replace them. Wahid apologized and promised it would never happen again. We trust Wahid and know that he feels badly and responsible.

The burglary presented us with an opportunity to appeal to the families for a contribution to the cost of the computer classes. We asked for $2 per month per student. Only five families have agreed to contribute so far. The failure of parents to support the education of their children continues to be a perplexing problem.

We could insist on payment from families who could afford to contribute and not allow their children to attend if they don't pay. There are two problems with this policy: Children would be punished for the failure of their parents, and no one would want the responsibility of determining which families can afford it and which can't. Imposing a fee and requiring classes to be self-supporting will have to wait for another day.

A MAJOR BREAKTHROUGH

Over a year ago we were asked to, and subsequently did, fund the cost of constructing a soccer field in the village of Quallah Loqman. We asked whether they could have one soccer program for boys and another for girls. I was told by a member of our staff it would not be possible to have a soccer program for girls: "Soccer is a boys' sport; they won't let girls play, girls can't be seen. Even if girls were allowed to play soccer, the field would need a surrounding wall to prevent men from watching."

Six weeks later I was sent photos of girls playing soccer without a wall. The headmistress of the girls' school was responsible for starting a soccer program for girls. This is nothing short of heroic.

Having fun and making a statement.

Flash forward to today. Reshkor, a village very near Quallah Loqman, asked us to fund additional after school math and science classes, a soccer field, and a soccer program for boys and girls. We agreed to fund all four. Reshkor's soccer program includes teams for younger and older girls. Quallah Loqman's program does not include teams for older girls.

When the headmistress of Quallah Loqman was asked whether they could add a soccer team for older girls, she said, "It's too soon. My village is not ready to accept a team for older girls, but as the younger girls get older, we will be able to have both." The girls who are playing soccer now will get older and her village will *de facto* end up with older girls playing soccer.

Quallah Loqman broke tradition by starting a soccer program for younger girls. Reshkor went a step further by establishing a soccer program for younger and older girls. In time, Quallah Loqman will have both. The annual cost of a soccer program is fifty dollars a month for a coach and one hundred dollars' worth of soccer balls and equipment. That is six hundred dollars a year to fund a major cultural breakthrough!

September Report from Kabul
Risk of Harm Continues to Rise

I'm looking out from our Intercontinental Hotel room window to the area where the Taliban launched an attack on this hotel three months ago. We arrived shortly after Burhanuddin Rabbani was killed by a suicide bomber and the US embassy was attacked. The hotel staff have given us very disturbing accounts of guests and staff killed during the attack and injuries suffered when guests jumped off high retaining walls and out of windows to avoid losing their lives.

We opted to stay in the Intercontinental Hotel even though it was attacked. Our theory was there will be more security and a second attack so close to the first is unlikely. Our assessment is not widely held. There are twenty-five guests and one hundred ninety-eight rooms. But, security is definitely greater and more thorough. When inspecting my suitcases, they discovered my Snickers Bars, Dots and Jujyfruits rolled up in socks. Very embarrassing!

Someone was killed inside the CIA building the night before a meeting we had with the US State Department. The CIA building is located across the street from where Nabi and I were dropped off and started our sprint to the US embassy. Tens of thousands have decided to remain indoors. The prevailing advice is to not go anywhere. People are afraid.

Why are we here when the risk of harm is so great? There are thousands of families and children now impacted by TIE's work.

Every visit, there are a few issues that only Nabi and I can resolve by being here. We are also able to discuss needs, goals and priorities with Basir for the following months. Finally, there is the reward factor. We're able to meet with and visit men, women and children who benefit from TIE's projects and programs. I wish every TIE supporter could visit someday. It's impossible to fully and adequately describe how important our work is.

Yesterday Nabi met with a friend who said he worried for our safety. He no longer worries about himself. He is "used to it." It struck me that to a certain extent I have become "used to terrorist attacks" over the past six years. They are like tragic automobile accidents. Streets are closed. Police and clean-up crews arrive and stop traffic. Several hours later, the streets reopen, and life on the street "returns to normal." "Life goes on" as before, except for those who are injured or killed and their families and friends. Everyone else eventually forgets what happened.

Fifty Dollars a Month—a Life Changer

On Sunday, we spent several hours with the street children sponsored through TIE. They are cleaner, healthier, better dressed, happier, and more confident every time we see them. Not one girl looks away or down or covers her face when I look her way. It has taken several years for most to feel comfortable looking me in the eye.

The same cannot be said of their mothers, most of whom wear burkas. One mother did, however, remove her veil, point to her daughter, and proudly announce, "I am spending all of the money on her education." Another pressed her hand to her heart and said to Nabi and me, "You have changed our lives." We're changing lives at a cost of half a yard per month—fifty dollars!

Going Solar

Following a speaking engagement in 2010, Jack Howell approached me and asked whether I knew anything about solar cooking. I had previously met with and visited Allart Ligtenberg in Los Altos, California. Allart has been providing solar energy solutions in Nepal for years. Both shared with me why they have become solar cooking devotees:

1. Two million people die a year due to smoke-inhalation illnesses caused by open fires. The majority who die are women because they do most of the cooking.
2. Deforestation is a major problem in most developing countries. Use of solar energy reduces the need for wood.
3. Women and children must often walk long distances to gather firewood, a task that may put them at risk and is exhausting.
4. Solar cookers can reach temperatures well in excess of 152 degrees, the temperature needed to pasteurize water. It's estimated that Afghans are drinking contaminated water 50 percent of the time.
5. Firewood is extremely expensive, and prohibitively so for some families. What they don't spend on cooking, they can spend on heating.

As with all new project advocates, I explained to Jack that I am not suffering from a lack of good ideas. I need people who will take responsibility for running the projects they recommend. He, unlike many others, didn't balk and thus began our solar cooking project.

It ultimately led to Jack and TIE receiving one of the world's most prestigious environmental awards in 2015 from the National Energy Globe. Jack could have received his recognition at a ceremony held in Tehran, Iran, in January 2016 but he decided not to go. Peer pressure is the reason most volunteers who have wanted to go with us to Afghanistan haven't gone. Jack had his share of pressure from his family but the factor that tipped the scale was the number of hours he'd be in transit, over twenty-five each way.

We began by enlisting volunteers who agreed to meet on weekends to construct solar ovens made of wood that could reach three hundred fifty to four hundred degrees Fahrenheit. Over a period of four months, crews ranging from fifteen to twenty volunteers constructed a hundred ovens. They were difficult and time-consuming to make and relatively costly. We needed an inexpensive cooker that was easy to make and Jack found the solution online: the "CooKit" developed by Solar Cookers International (SCI).

SCI has posted the pattern for a CooKit on its website making it accessible to everyone for free. These solar cookers are made of cardboard which we had stamped out by a box manufacturer. Then one side is covered with any suitable reflective material. They are light, can be folded to be easily stored, and can reach temperatures of two hundred fifty degrees.

The most expensive part of a CooKit is the reflective material, and we chose Mylar. Shortly after we had decided to make CooKits, Jack, while nursing a cup of coffee in a Peet's Coffee store, noticed a clerk pouring coffee beans into a bin. The beans were packaged in Mylar bags that were thrown away when empty. From that day forward, volunteers arranged to pick up the discarded coffee bags from several Peet's stores. Mylar overnight became free, and the cost of materials for a CooKit dropped below three dollars, and over sixty thousand Peet's coffee bags were rescued from becoming landfill.

Enter Interact District 5170

In 2013, I was contacted by Mariko Stenstedt, who was the international coordinator for Interact District 5170. Interact Clubs are affiliated with local Rotary Clubs and are established by students on high school campuses. After several e-mail exchanges, District 5170 decided to make TIE's solar CooKit their international project for the 2013–2014 school year.

The clubs raised enough funds for six thousand CooKits. They held work parties to clean and cut the mylar bags into patterns that were then stapled by hand to the cardboard CooKits. Each CooKit required one hundred seventy-five staples and nine Peet's Coffee bags. Six thousand CooKits therefore required approximately one million, fifty thousand staples and fifty-four thousand coffee bags.

I had no idea how much time it would take to make and distribute six thousand CooKits or how many people. To complete the stapling, we hired men in Afghanistan who did nothing but clean, cut, and staple Mylar onto the cardboard CooKits eight hours a day for several months.

One thing we knew we could not do is simply hand out CooKits and let families figure out how to use them. Serendipitously, I learned of and met Grace Magney, who lived in Kabul and, according to several sources, knows everything there is to know about solar. She offered to help by conducting solar cooking demonstrations and seminars. In May 2012, she sent me the following e-mail:

Hi Budd,

Today we had another great demonstration. Since I had successfully tested the CooKit at my house with rice, kidney beans, okra, onions, tomatoes, chicken legs and cake, I wanted to do a demonstration at TIE's office.

We put out twenty-two CooKits, and prepared two or three pots of each of the above. Rice and kidney beans take three hours, but vegetables and meat take only two so when I went over to TIE's office with all the prepared food, I had the rice and kidney pots into their oven bags and onto the CooKits by 8:30 a.m.; by 9:30 a.m. the first group of refugees had arrived.

Word came that the others who planned to attend had gone to a funeral and would arrive later. So, we started with the first group, showing them that the chicken and vegetables were truly raw and uncooked. They agreed. Then I had them help stir the cake; mixing together the dry ingredients I'd brought separately. Soon we had all the pots cooking in the CooKits.

While we waited, we discussed how it all works, letting the learners practice putting up and folding away a CooKit, and explaining the use of the central clothespin to determine the right adjustment toward the sun. They caught on to the clothespin immediately and proudly explained to each other how it worked. I've discovered that village people often grasp details like that and become absolutely dogmatic about them, which is good. Before the food was ready, more people came. In all there were twenty-five or so and we again explained the first steps.

At noon we opened all the oven bags and pots, and with steam pouring out, we filled plates and had a delicious, well-cooked meal together. Each family got a CooKit, three clothespins, an oven bag, and a pamphlet I had made of very easy Dari instructions to take home with them.

One of the men was a cook himself, and because of his great interest and keen mind, we gave him three CooKits, saying he had to advertise it to others, show how it worked and spread the desire to have one.

Everything went well. Today in the sun was a lot hotter than when I did the first demonstration last October and soon we were all looking for a shady place to sit in the garden or porch. It was a wonderful day promoting solar cooking. I thoroughly enjoyed it.

Best Regards,
Grace

Eliminating smoke with solar.

SOLAR COOKING CLASSES BEGIN

Following Grace's demonstrations, Karim, one of our guards, was hired to provide solar cooking classes in refugee camps. We also hired the cook Grace described, to teach the sixty-one families living in his camp. Cookits are simple devices, but it's very important to prove that they work and to explain why cooking with solar is so important to a family's health. Karim eventually taught solar cooking classes in nineteen refugee camps to over three thousand families.

Photos of Karim's first solar cooking class arrived by e-mail. Not one woman was in the photos: women weren't being allowed or invited to attend. I had mistakenly assumed that they would be there since they do most of the cooking. Thereafter, we insisted women be allowed and invited, so soon their attendance rose and over time became common. Any opportunity we have to include women when and where they normally wouldn't go, we seize.

One concern from the beginning of this project was whether the CooKits would become fuel for the fire. After all, it takes two to three hours to cook a meal and Jack and Allart are the only people I know willing to start cooking that far in advance of a meal. Basir visited several camps two weeks after solar classes had been given to see whether the CooKits were being used. Not only were they, but families that hadn't taken the class wanted to know when we would be offering another.

Cost Sharing Fails Again

When visiting families, Basir learned that many didn't have good cooking pots. He said they had "no lids, they were flimsy, and they weren't black." Black absorbs sun rays; lighter colors don't. We offered to split the cost for seven-dollar black pots that Basir had located in a bazaar. The unanimous response was, "We're too poor." The only way to determine if in fact a family is too poor is to wait them out. Nobody came forward within ten days of the offer.

We were faced with two competing objectives: the desire to share the cost and the need to prove that the CooKits worked. While waiting, Maiward was able to find an alternative black aluminum pot for four dollars and still no one offered to share the cost.

We bought fifty pots for two hundred dollars. This was enough to provide proof of concept. After the fifty had been distributed, we provided brushes and black paint. They painted their own pots black during the lessons.

The CooKits became so popular we began giving each family two. One is not enough to cook all they needed for a meal. Assuming an average family of ten, there are now thirty thousand Afghan refugees who know how to cook with solar, and can.

WAPIs

Another device Jack taught volunteers how to make is a water-pasteuri-zation indicator (WAPI). It's a small device that hangs from the edge of a pot filled with water and is essentially a thermometer with a material inside that melts at one hundred fifty-two degrees Fahrenheit. When it melts, the water is rid of all bacteria harmful to a human being: it is "clean" or "pasteurized." Volunteers have made so many WAPIs that we lost count. It is well over seven thousand.

I always thought that even if the CooKits and WAPIs served no other purpose than pasteurizing water, Jack's project would be a success. We now know that Afghan families are cooking their food and pasteurizing water using their CooKits—a home run! One father proudly reported his family was saving forty cents a day, twelve dollars a month on their cost of wood. Is that significant? He wouldn't have gone out of his way to tell us if it wasn't.

Ignore Solar!

On September 10, 2011, Hilary Clinton said, in announcing the creation of a multimillion stove cooker project:

"I am very excited to tell you about a new initiative that will…help put vital new tools in the hands of millions of people. As we meet here in New York, women are cooking dinner for their families in homes and villages around the world. As many as 3 billion people are gathering around open fires or old and inefficient stoves in small kitchens and poorly ventilated houses. Many of the women have labored over these hearths for hours, often with their infant babies strapped to their backs, and they have spent many more hours gathering the fuel. The food they prepare is different on every continent, but the air they breathe is shockingly similar—a toxic mix of chemicals released by burning wood or other solid fuel that can reach two hundred times the amount that our EPA considers safe for breathing…

The World Health Organization considers smoke from dirty stoves to be one of the five most serious health risks that face people in poor developing countries. Nearly two million people die from its effects each year, which is more than twice the number who die from malaria. Because the smoke contains greenhouse gasses such as carbon dioxide and methane, as well as black carbon, it also contributes to climate change." [6]

Thus began the Global Alliance for Clean Cookstoves. It's now reportedly a 250-million-dollar project. Jack Howell wrote to determine if the Alliance would be interested in contributing to our solar cooker project. Why not, he reasoned. Solar ovens are one hundred per cent effective against the smoke inhalation problem and eliminate the need for costly fuel. Jack received this response:

"Dear Mr. Howell,

Thank you for your note to the Alliance. Unfortunately, we are not providing funds for deployment grants at this time as our initial focus is on standards and testing, health and climate research, advocacy and awareness, development of new business models, and the removal of barriers to wide scale implementation. You might try your local Rotary Club for a grant as I have heard they are providing grants for stove projects in some states. USAID/ Kabul might also be a source of funding for your project. I wish you all the best in your important work."

How much time and money will it take to "establish standards and testing, conduct climate and health research, develop new business models, and study how to remove barriers to wide scale implementation?" Why not spend that time and money on successful projects and programs already in existence?

I'm increasingly convinced of the superior advantage of small-scale grass roots projects and organizations. They "just do it" and if it works, do it again. If it doesn't, they experiment until something does. Large bureaucratic organizations spend too much time and money studying problems that can easily be solved through trial and error.

It's worth noting that the Global Alliance for Clean Cookstoves has not and will not spend a single dollar on solar cooking or cookers. They are only interested in projects that make wood and fuel burning stoves more efficient. Solar cookers are 100% efficient, don't generate any smoke, don't require any wood, and are infinitely better for the atmosphere than fuel burning stoves. Solar cookers also cost much less to build. We've written to them asking why they are ignoring solar cookers and had no response.

CHAPTER 11

Events in 2012
Public Recognition

❖　❖　❖

I RECEIVED CONTRA COSTA'S 2012 Humanitarian award. I, more than anyone else, know that this award belongs to hundreds of volunteers and con-
tributors who have made everything possible. I just happen to be driving
the bus with aspirations of becoming a passenger someday.

NEWSWORTHY?

Rudyard Kipling wrote the poem, *If*: "If you can keep your head when all
about you are losing theirs…"[7] I recall first reading that poem in a high
school graduation card sent to me by my grandmother, Gladys. She kept
her head for ninety-six years and lived up to her name. Yes, Gladys is the
contraction of two words.

Five American soldiers recently burned Korans at the Bagram military base outside Kabul, thereby igniting the most extreme factions within and outside Afghanistan. American soldiers could be killed over this
thoughtless act.

Why was there so much news coverage? Why was there any? Must all
inflammatory actions and words be broadcast around the world? People

are losing their heads because they are being filled with news reports of extreme actions and ideologies. One thoughtless act inspires others. Did the world really need to know about Korans being burned by American soldiers? I didn't.

KNITTERS IN PUYALLUP, WASHINGTON

Hats off to Vickie Ghulam and members of the LDS church Pleasant Hill First Ward. They have knitted and donated hundreds of hats to TIE that are now keeping children's heads warm in Afghanistan. Vickie also enlisted her sister, Elizabeth La Rue Thomas, and Elizabeth's daughter, Rebecca. They managed to make knitting hats one of three service projects at the Puyallup South State Women's Conference. Puyallup is, by the way, the name of an Indian tribe living along the Puget Sound (thank you, Google). I'm told two hundred hats are on their way to us.

APRIL TRIP CANCELLED

If it hadn't been for the recent attacks by the Taliban, Nabi and I would be in Dubai now, having completed a sixteen-hour flight from San Francisco. Tomorrow we would have been on a three-hour flight to Kabul. The word on the ground is that there are too many roadblocks, streets closed, and checkpoints, making travel in Kabul even worse.

Many organizations and government agencies have gone into "lock down" mode and are just beginning to reopen. Basir reports from Kabul that Afghans are staying inside, refusing to go anywhere, thereby limiting the number of meetings we could have. We'll go when conditions on the ground permit. Our work is too important for us to stop going.

OUR MOST PROMISING STUDENT

Three years ago, Mir Hussein, one of the seventy-two children sponsored through TII. Last November, he graduated fifth in his class from high school. He passed the national entrance exam for college and is waiting to learn whether and where he will go. Mir is blind but has not been attending a school for the blind. His brother accompanies him to school every day. Mir's brother told us he helps him with his eyes, and Mir helps him with his homework. From selling pencils on the streets to fifth in his class and on to college in three years, all made possible by a support payment of fifty dollars a month!

Education, the solution for almost everything.

NINE YEARS LATER AND STILL UNSCATHED

When first raising funds to build the school in Lalander, I was asked on more than one occasion, "What are you going to do if the Taliban blow it up?" My response then and still is, "They will build it again." Afghans are relentless in fighting for what they believe is right and the vast majority support educating girls.

It's nine years later, and we have not had one attack or threat against any of our teachers or our offices. There are thousands who know who we are and where our office is located. If they wanted to drive us out, we would have known by now. Is it possible we've earned a hall pass or are we just one of Aesop's geese that lays golden eggs that they have decided not to kill.

A MOTHER HOLDS A PACKING PARTY

When we hold a packing party, over 100 volunteers show up to pack. Schools, churches, mosques and individuals all bring clothing. Here's what one organizer wrote about the Indian Valley Elementary school's collection:

"This month's theme for my daughter's Clover Club was 'Making the World a Better Place.' What better opportunity to highlight the refugee problem in Afghanistan and include the whole school in a donation drive? Our school was very generous with their donations, and we collected many pairs of soccer cleats for the TIE sponsored girls' soccer teams in addition to pounds of clothes.

Fifteen six-year-olds came to my house and sorted the clothes and even learned how to fold (this is a skill that will definitely come in handy around my house). Then they packed the boxes and labeled them with the help of several other mothers. In all we have over twenty boxes of clothing, shoes and stuffed animals that will surely help the refugees in Afghanistan.

The experience was memorable for the girls. Iris, one of our Clovers, said, "I feel sad for the people who have nothing, but I feel a little bit happy that we are sending clothes. I really wish I could bring them more sun so they wouldn't be so cold."

Our Favorite "Nut"

Patti Bauernfeind just dedicated a 28.5-mile swim to TIE! The start and finish of the swim will be at Battery Park, not far from Ground Zero and across the river from the Statue of Liberty. She must swim without a wetsuit, cannot touch the boat that escorts her, and will feed or eat every twenty minutes by drinking an endurance sports drink while floating on her back. Patti already holds the world record for swimming twenty-one miles across Lake Tahoe (10 hours 38 minutes in 67-degree water). She was also a member of the only all women's relay team that swam to the Farallon Islands off San Francisco in 20 foot swells and 50-degree water.

Who are these people? Most people I know, including me, need an electric pump to inflate a swim mattress.

Patti wrote the following to her friends: "Some have questioned my sanity around this swim due to the distance and reputation of the East and Harlem Rivers in terms of water quality. Admittedly, it is a bit nutty. However, this swim is very meaningful to me and allows me to raise money for an important cause—supporting education and promoting peace in Afghanistan.

I love swimming and am thrilled to be able to tie my love of open water swimming with my drive to help educate kids in Afghanistan. My father grew up just outside New York City. I have memories of being mesmerized by the Statue of Liberty, which is the universal symbol for welcoming refugees and for providing opportunities to those who have suffered in other countries.

Through my tutoring of Selab, a 17-year-old Afghan refugee, I learned of the dire state of schools in Afghanistan. He and his family are very grateful to be here and to have a future. There are millions of children who aren't as lucky. I am supporting Trust in Education, an organization that has been committed to educating Afghan children for over nine years."

As for Patti feeling a "little nutty," we can relate. We, after all, believe we can bring about change in a society that is most often portrayed as intractable. The fact is, we know people can make a meaningful difference if they have Patti's patience, endurance, resolve and passion.

They are Ours!

TIE recently loaned Aqa Ali Shams fifteen computers to establish a computer lab. Establishing and maintaining the computers as ours is very important. Not all schools are willing to accept the premise that they are "ours," except when they need to be repaired. We don't want anyone having the right to decide they should be somewhere else. They also shouldn't sit idle. That happened in one village when parents stopped paying for the gasoline needed to run the generator that powered the computers. We removed the computers and took them to another village.

While on the subject of computers I have some advice for techies who want to make a difference in education. There is enough hardware capability already. What the world needs is educational software that is user friendly and preferably free or easily affordable.

There's more to report, but it stopped raining and the hatch has begun. For you city folk, that means grab your fly rod and head for the river. The hatch waits for no one. Yes, I'm in Montana working on what once was "the book" and has now become "the damn book." I had no idea how difficult or time consuming this would be.

ACTS OF COURAGE

Nabi sent me this article today. It ties right into our play strategy, which includes funding soccer and volleyball programs for girls. Athletic programs for girls enable brave girls and their families to break through barriers that have existed for hundreds of years. They will help redefine what a girl and woman can and may do.

August 2, 2012
Radio Free Europe/Radio Liberty

"Afghanistan's only female Olympian does not expect to win a medal, but says the opportunity to compete in London is worth more than gold. Sprinter Tahmina Kohestani, who will compete in the 100 meters says the real prize will be to see more Afghan women enter the sporting arena in the future. 'If I can open the way or motivate other Afghan girls to join us and improve the quality of your sports...I think that is worth more to me than a medal.'Kohestani, yet to break 14 seconds in her event, far off the favorite's times, has broken taboos at a record pace in her home country. 'To reach my training every day...I had to take three different buses. On every bus, people were bothering me and speaking harshly because they thought it was against their honor, if I, as a Muslim Afghan girl, represented Afghanistan in the games.' On one occasion, a driver kicked her off his bus. 'That day I trained with tears in my eyes,' she said. 'Now I work hard in order to promote the culture of sport among my people.'

Tahmina is only the third Afghan woman ever to have earned the opportunity to compete in the Olympic Games. 'I will wear a headscarf, long trousers, and a blouse with long sleeves,' she said. 'I will run in clothes that my trainers and the head of Afghan National Committee advise me to wear. It is completely Islamic.'" [8]

OCTOBER REPORT FROM AFGHANISTAN
IMPACT OF ATTACK ON MALALA YOUSAFZAI

Nabi and I arrived in Kabul on Sunday. As we left the airport we drove by an area where a woman launched a suicide attack several weeks earlier. Everything appeared normal except for the number of police protecting the airport.

I asked Basir what impact the attack on Malala Yousafzai had had on Afghanistan. Malala is the fourteen-year-old girl who was recently attacked by members of the Taliban while riding a school bus in Swat Valley, Pakistan. She was shot because she had become an influential advocate of women's rights. The Taliban proudly and publicly took credit for the attack. They also vowed to go after her and her father if she survives.

At the suggestion of the Minister of Education, every Afghan student attending school on Saturday prayed for Malala. Could this horrific attack possibly be a catalyst for a cooperative worldwide effort to rid the planet of these sadistic extremists? There are indications that villagers are banding together to do just that.

Several weeks ago, villagers in southern Afghanistan fought Taliban extremists living in their area. They were fed up with the extent to which the Taliban were interfering with their lives. Girls' schools had been destroyed and lives were lost defending the right of girls to be educated. Encouraging reports are surfacing of private militias taking control of many areas once controlled by the Taliban.

Delivering Buckets from the Brigade Nabi and I are here in part because we find ourselves in the middle of a war for gender equality that would be difficult to wage entirely from home. For example, tomorrow we will meet with the Ministry of Education to make certain the school being built for girls in Farza opens next March. If we are successful, two hundred and fifty girls will be out of dilapidated, unsafe classrooms, off the floor, and sitting in new desks.

Trust in Education is essentially a bucket brigade comprised almost entirely of volunteers bringing supplies to people risking their lives for basic human rights. We provide schools, teachers, classes, learning centers, playgrounds, books, libraries, soccer programs, computers, food, shoes, bedding and clothing. I can honestly report to you from the front line that we are making tremendous progress—particularly in educating girls. If we weren't, Nabi and I would be home.

Today has been very productive and tomorrow promises to be better. Nabi is going out to dinner with a friend and I will watch cricket games on a snowy TV screen. Fortunately, my supply of Snickers bars and apples is plentiful.

SKYPE BRIDGES THE GAP

We arranged a Skype encounter between Corte Madera students and four Afghan children they have been sponsoring for several years. Due to the eleven and half hour time zone time difference, the Afghan children came to our office after dark, a risk they willingly took to meet their sponsors.

With plenty of technical interruptions, the children, on both ends, learned they share more in common than not, except for their living conditions. Corte Madera students experienced the joy and reward of meeting children whose lives they've changed. They wrote the following about their Skype encounter:

"During the Trust in Education video chat I felt excited. I felt excited because I was meeting new people, and these people were across the world. I also felt nervous. I have a lot of pressure by modeling good behavior for the kids. This was really fun to talk to the kids in Afghanistan."—Nick

"I loved talking with the kids who we raised money for, and it made me feel good inside. It was cool to see kids we have helped for a while. I love doing projects, art and baking to help the kids to get off the streets."—Riley

"I felt like they really needed me, and I felt like, well, I felt really good about it. I can't even explain how happy I felt. It helped me see how much it mattered to them."—Olivia

"Today was a magical day for me. I got to meet four students who Corte Madera raises money for. One of them loves chicken."—Meghan

"Today, we Skyped with Budd MacKenzie and some kids in Afghanistan. It felt really good to know that the money we raised selling baked goods and walking dogs paid for their education. They seemed really happy that they got to go to school. Some of the kids would be out on the streets begging and selling small things to support all of their brothers and sisters if they weren't in school."—Christy

Note: Afghans are not "Afghanis." They are Afghans. Their currency is expressed in Afghanis. This took seven months for me to discover. Afghans are too polite to correct us.

CHAPTER 12

Events in 2013
Another Eagle Scout
Candidate Steps In

❖ ❖ ❖

AFGHAN SCHOOLS HAVE COMPUTER CLASSES taught without computers. A Boy Scout has offered to come to the rescue. Will Goldie, a high school junior at Acalanes in Lafayette, contacted me offering to assemble and provide us with Raspberry Pi computers as his Eagle Scout project. Raspberry Pi computers are the size of a mobile phone and cost less than forty-five dollars to build. He'll raise the money and take responsibility for the entire project. We can ship the computers to Afghanistan through the Denton program and support more computer classes. Thousands of Afghan students will benefit as a result.

OCTOBER REPORT FROM KABUL.
SCHOOL FOR GIRLS OPENS IN FARZA
Three years from conception, the school for girls in the village of Farza finally opened to two hundred and fifty girls and forty boys. Built with ninety-two thousand dollars of materials supplied by TIE and volunteer labor supplied by the villagers, it's our first partnership with Farza. There

will be more. Desks for the school were provided by the Million Dollar Roundtable Foundation and students at Corte Madera school in Los Altos, California.

This year's enrollment is three hundred and seventy girls, one hundred and twenty more than were enrolled before the school opened. The resistance to allowing girls to attend school is falling. A major challenge now is finding solutions for girls who have "aged out." They cannot enroll until they qualify for their appropriate grade level.

We were told by a teacher that it's much easier to enroll students than when he first began. "In the beginning villagers didn't allow their sons or daughters to go to school. Schools were perceived to be 'places where children were taught to be non-believers'." It would be interesting to know what impact, if any, education has had on all religions. Is there, in fact, a correlation between education and a decline in religious followers? Shouldn't the opposite occur in Afghanistan where religion is an integral part of every school's curriculum? In any event, things are much better now. The vast majority want every child to attend school.

WOULD WE BUILD ANOTHER SCHOOL?

In November 2010, Shane O'Brien handed me a phone message. Zohra Aziz had called asking whether TIE could contribute to the cost of building a school for girls in her village, Farza. I asked Shane to call her back and explain why we couldn't. Several minutes later, Shane was still busy, so I decided to call. Several times during the next three years, I felt it had been a mistake. Had Shane made the call, there would have been one less project and considerably less blood pressure medication.

Zohra explained that her family had left her village when she was five and returned twenty years later. Farza had schools for boys but not for girls. Girls were being taught inside villagers' homes. Girls begged Zohra to raise money to build a school for them; she had been trying for two years but hadn't had much success.

When we raised money for the school built in Lalander, several who hadn't contributed were concerned that the Taliban would destroy it. The school in Farza would be built with volunteer labor; I knew that if volunteers built it, they would defend it. In fact, one villager did, putting his life at risk.

In June 2011, Farim, an unarmed night guard at the construction site, stood his ground against an armed attack. He spent a week in the hospital recovering from his injuries and resumed his post when he returned. He was earning three dollars a day as the guard, a clear testament to Afghan resolve.

When I first learned of the attack, I'd assumed it was because the school would be for girls, but that wasn't the issue. Walid Osman, an Afghan who has supported TIE in many ways, had, midway through construction, arranged for the donation of a dome-shaped, fiberglass classroom powered with solar panels. It could be installed and relocated easily and cost less than ten thousand dollars. The money we paid to build a four classroom school could have purchased nine dome classrooms.

A religious leader in the area had concluded that any domed structure was an affront to Islam; in his view, the shape was only for mosques. The dome was severely damaged during the attack, not repaired, and ultimately removed. It's fortunate that we hadn't known about the dome classrooms before construction of the school began. We might have bought domes. If we had, they would have been destroyed.

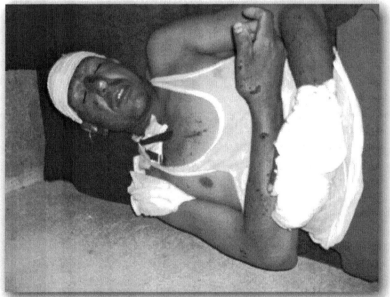

He protected the dome classroom without a weapon.

Other advantages of the project were that the Afghan government would pay the school's operating costs and students would receive academic credit for the classes they took. The school in Lalander was not accredited for several years after its construction.

The villagers in Lalander had suspected that the project manager hired by Central Asia Institute to build and run the school had purposely delayed accreditation because once the government took over, he would lose his position as headmaster. He maintained that the government had slowed the accreditation process because it wanted Central Asia Institute to continue paying the teachers' salaries and operating expenses. Both suspicions may have been correct, but the project manager had no credibility with the villagers I met. He had, after all, built a house for himself during the construction of the school using the same workers and materials.

The construction of the school in Farza fit all our criteria. It would be a school for girls, accredited, managed by the Afghan government, and be built by the villagers. The men who built it would protect it. Finally, the catalyst for making it happen would be an educated and accomplished Afghan woman who was a role model for every girl in the village.

Having now funded and overseen the successful construction of one school, Nabi and I would not do it again. It took too long to build and there were too many bureaucratic obstacles to overcome. On more than one occasion, construction had stopped, putting completion at significant risk. It is also questionable today whether it was the best use of ninety-two thousand dollars.

TIE has for several years provided classes in Math, Science, Computers, English, Art, and Literacy before and after school and during winter vacation. This program now employs twenty-four teachers teaching well over 1300 students at a cost of less than thirty thousand dollars a year. Classes are easy to establish, popular, and are welcomed everywhere we've gone, without any red tape. Classes held in homes and in TIE's learning centers also make it possible for girls to be educated who wouldn't be otherwise. We're best suited to helping existing schools, establishing learning centers, and providing alternative means of learning outside schools.

Building schools is for those who have plenty of money and time. We have neither. Moreover, a building does not an education make. Qualified teachers, books, school supplies, a place to meet, and children eager to learn do. None of these component parts is expensive.

A WISH LIST PROJECT THAT SAVES LIVES

Before leaving Farza, we were led to a small stream that eight hundred children must cross daily on their way to and from school. In the spring when the snow melts it is dangerous—so dangerous, one young girl drowned trying to cross. Building a footbridge over the water was their number one wish and it had to be done before winter set in and while the stream was shallow. We agreed to pay the cost of materials before we left. They will build it.

A SOLUTION IS FOUND

We visited Aqa Ali Shams, a school for girls located in Kabul. We'd previously installed fifteen computers in one of its classrooms, effectively creating a computer lab. Today we discovered that each child able to use the lab had only thirty minutes a week!

There are two problems preventing the students from having more lab time. First, the size of the school: six thousand students. Second, the school is required to teach seventeen subjects. Students attend school for four hours a day, six days a week. Thirty minutes a week is the amount of time the principal could take away from the other classes and 'squeeze in' for the fewer than five hundred students lucky enough to have lab time.

Before we left, we discussed the possibility of providing winter computer classes when "school is out." School administrators are required to work in the schools during the winter break, and there are plenty of classrooms available. We'll be able to provide computer classes that are 90 minutes long and given six days a week. The principal agreed to work from her end to make this possible.

Crowd Funding Pays Off

Will Goldie set out to raise $2,500 for his Raspberry Pi computer project using Indiegogo, a crowdfunding website. Raspberry Pi was so enthusiastic about this project it agreed to match donations up to a total of ten thousand dollars. I just received word by email from Will that he has raised twenty thousand! Once again we've been able to serve as a link between people who want to help and those who need it. We TIE'd another one. By the way, that is how the name Trust in Education was chosen. The acronym came first, then the name. The vision from the outset was to connect communities and people and tie them together.

CHAPTER 13

Events in 2014
After we Leave

❖ ❖ ❖

SEVERAL PEOPLE HAVE ASKED WHAT will happen when our troops leave this year. During our last visit, I asked Farza's village leader the same question. He smiled and said, "No one can predict the future of Afghanistan." It's true. That is why Afghans are fond of saying *Inshallah* (God willing) when referring to the future.

A village leader in Tangi Saidan, while concerned about Afghanistan's future, thought it would be best if American troops left. He agrees with many Americans that it's time for Afghanistan to move toward self-sufficiency. "Our economy and too many Afghans are dependent upon foreigners. We're becoming lazy," he said.

His primary concern is whether the Afghan military will have enough men, weapons and supplies to defeat the Taliban. "We can defend our country," he said. Afghans have throughout history proved that they can. Whether they will receive enough financial support during the transition from dependency to self-sufficiency is the question.

SCOUTS STEP UP AGAIN

One purpose of TIE's newsletters is to share our experiences, observations, trials and tribulations when working in Afghanistan. Another is to report on accomplishments of TIE supporters. I responded to two "What can we do?" requests from students, suggesting they make ladderball games.

An Acalanes high school student, Matthew Armstrong, in search of an Eagle Scout project and a Girl Scout troop in Portola Valley took on the project. Between them they made 50 ladderball games that are presently being distributed to refugee camps and schools in Kabul.

The game, though easy to play, is difficult to explain. You'll need to "Google" it. Google can be used as a verb, can't it? Reports from Kabul are that they "love the game," and it is great for schools that don't have much playground space. Aqa Ali Shams is allowing teachers to bring the game into their classrooms.

Ladderball comes to Afghanistan

My Fifteeen Minutes

In 1999, during a private audience with His Holiness, the Dalai Lama, Dick Grace shared "the kernel of an idea" he had been formulating: "Wouldn't it be wonderful if we could do a better job of transforming our contemplative practice into compassionate action?" His Holiness enthusiastically embraced the idea, replying, "We have to work on that."

Dick gathered friends and philanthropic angels willing to help him shine the light on the healing power of compassion in action. From his inspiration, the first Unsung Heroes of Compassion event was created in 2001, with subsequent events held in 2005 and 2009.

I had an opportunity to meet His Holiness, the Dalai Lama, having been chosen as one of 51 "Unsung Heroes" this year. While honored, I also felt uncomfortable with the recognition. TIE is the sum of its parts, and I am only one.

Before the award ceremony, I watched every Netflix movie and read every article I could find about Buddhism, Tibet, and "His Holiness." He has spent his entire life reflecting, responding to admirers, and in fear for his life. When he walked into the banquet room of the hotel, for the first time in my life I experienced "aura." It's impossible to describe. You'll recognize it when it passes by.

The start of my fifteen minutes.

As far as being an "unsung hero," praises are directed my way more often than is comfortable. One that was life altering occurred during my second trip to Afghanistan in 2005. We were explaining our sewing program to a visibly weathered and scarred elderly Afghan woman. Her daughter had been accepted into the program. She asked whether another of her daughters could be admitted. We explained that we could accept only one per family to maximize the number of families we could help. Although disappointed, she looked into my eyes, raised both arms into the air, pointed to the sky and said, "God has sent you to us." It was at that moment I knew how important and rewarding this work would be. I have thought of her often since.

My awakening began with her.

Immediately following the Unsung Hero luncheon, I returned home, tried to walk on water, and sank immediately to the bottom of the pool. My fifteen minutes of fame were over, and I was soaking wet.

Corrupt Governments Cost Less

I recently returned from a visit to China and read about an interesting phenomenon concerning corrupt governments. The Chinese government is cracking down on corruption. As a consequence, fewer people are applying for government jobs and government employees are quitting at a higher rate. There were twenty-five per cent fewer applicants for government positions in one area.

Governments compete with the private sector for employees. Corrupt governments can pay less and attract more employees than those that aren't. It never occurred to me that corrupt governments are less expensive to maintain.

They Just Keep Coming!

TIE recently distributed five thousand hand-knitted sweaters, scarves, hats and mittens to Afghan children and their families thanks to Ann Rubin and the nonprofit organization, Afghans for Afghans. Ann for years has developed and organized a cadre of knitters throughout the United States who, at her urging, agreed to knit for Afghan families.

All They Needed Was a Chance

Qudsia, Basir's better half, is responsible for our sponsorship program. She provides assistance to the children and their families and serves as the intermediary between children and their sponsors. We asked her to profile a few sponsored children:

Anil, born in 1997, has seven brothers and sisters all living in two rooms. He was selling chewing gum on the streets of Kabul before being sponsored in 2010. He's in the 8th grade and ranked 2nd in his class of forty-five students. According to Qudsia, "He is a very smart boy, loves to read, play cricket and soccer. His friends love him because he always has a smile on his face. He doesn't complain, believes life is very short and everyone should enjoy each moment."

Nelab, born in 1999, is in the 9th grade and ranked first in her class of thirty-five students. When she was very young her father was killed during a Taliban suicide attack in Kabul. Her mother washes clothes to support her family. Her mother says, "Nelab is a very strong girl, and despite the family's challenges, she never gives up."

Najeebullah was born in 1997, is in the 10th grade, and ranked 10th in his class of fifty-two students. He sold books on the streets of Kabul before his sponsorship began. Now he spends that time on his studies. He wants to become a doctor and "be good to my society."

Rabia, born in 1998, is in the 9th grade and previously sold chewing gum on the streets, and is ranked sixth in her class of fifty-two students. "She lives with her mother, father and six siblings in three rooms. Her father is a soldier and often away. She worries about her father."

The vast majority of the sponsored students I've interviewed want to be teachers. Teachers are held in very high esteem. It's one profession they recognize "helps their country." Contrast that with how few American students want to be teachers or express the need to help their country. Our value system could use some tweaking. Others might argue we need an overhaul.

RESCUED DOGS GET PUPPY CHOW

As some may recall, two pallets of dog food were included in our last shipment. It arrived and has been delivered to Nowzad, a nonprofit organization in Kabul that provides medical care for injured strays. Nowzad also helps reunite soldiers with dogs they've adopted or cared for while in Afghanistan.

Soldiers are not allowed to befriend a dog, but they do. Reuniting a soldier with his dog has proven to be helpful in overcoming post-traumatic stress disorder. Families of soldiers who have died in Afghanistan have also been able to arrange transportation of their child's dog to their loved ones. Nowzad has the only authorized animal shelters in Afghanistan.

Americans are, according to several Afghans, much more affectionate in the treatment of their dogs than Afghans. There isn't much cuddling between a dog and its owner.

Afghans own dogs primarily for security. They're four-legged alarm systems and protectors. Why would dogs become "man's best friend" in our world and not theirs? Shouldn't unconditional love naturally flow between humans and their dogs everywhere in the world?

Pen Farthing, the founder of Nowzad, on the right, knows what a dog can do for soldiers and their families.

WHAT DO WE DO?

The shipment of dog food reminds me of how difficult it has become to answer the question: "What does Trust in Education do?" No one has the attention span for a complete answer. A full response would include: TIE provides before and after school classes to over thirteen hundred children (more than fifty percent girls), funded the construction of two schools and five learning centers, funds computer classes, made and distributed thousands of solar cookers and WAPI's (water purification devices), purchased and distributed over twenty three thousand fruit trees, funded three irrigation systems, two foot bridges and two wells, sponsors seventy-five street children, collected and packed tens of thousands of pounds of clothing and rice donated by Stop Hunger Now (enough for 1.3 million meals), installs playground equipment, supports soccer and volleyball programs, and helped deliver dog food to Afghanistan's only authorized animal shelter.

The short answer is: TIE provides and does what it can, always bearing in mind its most important mission is to help educate children in Afghanistan. Education is the long-term solution to almost everything and an increasing cadre of volunteers have made it possible to do much more.

Our World and Theirs

I'm in Montana laboring over this book again. Tammy Miller's homemade triple berry pie is fifteen feet away. One hundred fifty feet away is a river where we "tube." Tubing, for you city folk, is sitting on an inner tube, derriere held above the rocks below, relying on the river current to transport you downstream. It is a slow lazy float through nature. My nature scorecard currently includes sighting three bears, two eagles, a water snake, and more deer and geese than can be counted.

Go tubing, eat triple-berry pie, play outdoors or write? That has been the question every summer. It explains why it is taking this long to finish.

Montana should be on everyone's bucket list, particularly Glacier National Park. Don't procrastinate. The glaciers will, according to whoever predicts these things, be gone by 2030. Montana has lakes, rivers, and streams too numerous to count, blue skies, friendly people who have time to talk, farmland with an array of colors, and excellent family owned restaurants. It's a perfect place to throttle down during the summer. The locals have a saying that describes conditions here: "We have nine months of winter and three months of guests."

If I weren't writing, I'd be kayaking down this river.

What does any of this have to do with TIE? Moments ago I received an email from Basir, our director in Kabul. He is picking up our most recent shipment at the Kabul airport. Waiting at the airport cargo gate for three to four hours before being allowed in is not uncommon. On one occasion they waited five hours only to be told to return another day. In addition, Taliban attacked the airport a few days ago. He and those who accompany him are putting their lives at risk to pick up our shipment.

MONTANA POLICE BLOTTER

Now, next to me is a paper containing entries in the Kalispell police blotter which I read this morning. Compare and contrast calls to the police here with what Basir faces everyday. My comments are bracketed.

10:11 a.m.—"Two small diaper-wearing children escaped while their grandpa took a nap. They were returned home." (It could, of course, have been worse if the children had been napping and Grandpa was found wandering in his diaper.)

9:25 p.m.—"A potentially intoxicated man stood in his yard and yelled angrily at people as they drove by his house." (He's "mad as Hell and not going to take it anymore." What's a potentially intoxicated person? Doesn't everyone have that potential?)

1:26 p.m.—"Someone called 911 to report that four or five kids were jumping off a bridge into a river. The caller was advised that nothing illegal had occurred." (In Montana, if you want to jump off a bridge, go for it. The strong will survive.)

5:51 p.m.—"A man was seen driving in an unnatural and potentially unsafe position." (What is an "unnatural and potentially unsafe driving position?" The imagination runs wild.)

8:05 p.m.—"Neighbors argued excessively over the state of a shared fence. They agreed to discontinue conversations involving the fence." (Good fences make good neighbors according to Robert Frost. They must have a bad fence.)

11:20 p.m.—"A man said a log in the water was hitting his dock. He requested that a deputy come remove the log. His request was denied." (I don't suppose they would consider chasing the geese off my lawn every morning. They are after all trespassers eating my grass and using my lawn as a dumping ground.)

3:05 p.m.—"Reportedly a pack of children were drinking beer at a local lake." (Is a pack of children six or 12?)

7:43 p.m.—"Someone called in after picking up a three-year-old who was riding his Big Wheel down Highway 93. The toddler was returned home." (On the road again! Born to be free!)

Here I sit, laptop on lap, pie at the ready, watching the Swan River flow by, reading my email and typing excerpts from the Kalispell police blotter. Every now and then I am reminded of how fortunate I am and we are. That's what all this has to do with Afghanistan. Not every connection is made with a straight line.

OCTOBER REPORT FROM AFGHANISTAN

We arrived in Kabul one luggage bag short, the one with my clothing. Fortunately, the bag with candy for the children and my Sees chocolates made it. If the lost bag doesn't arrive soon, I'll have them make me a burqa.

That would be an interesting sight, me in a burqa walking behind Nabi, pretending to be his wife. He of course would be wearing his favorite Hawaiian shirt. Nabi, by the way, loves animals as much as they love him.

That's as close as Nabi was willing to be. Donkey felt the same.

CAN WE BLAME THEM?

Today we held a solar cooking class at our office in Kabul. We had asked a refugee camp leader to send couples or women. The bus we'd provided to bring them to the office arrived without a single woman on board. Nabi, Basir and I had to decide what to do. Should we go forward with the cooking lesson or not? They had not done what we'd requested and why provide cooking lessons to men who in all likelihood don't do the cooking?

Basir spoke with the camp leader and told him we were taking the men back to camp and the bus should be reloaded with women, children and no more than three men. Two hours later the bus was back with the mix we'd prescribed. We won this test of wills. We don't always.

The solar cooking class went well, followed by a lesson on how to play ladder ball. This too went well. Then we started distributing clothing and a bucket of rice to each family. The day went downhill from there.

We were told there were families waiting outside our gate who should be allowed in. The gate was opened slightly and people began pushing their way in. Many were children of the women who were already inside. One woman who had brought two children insisted that her children and she each receive a bucket of rice. A woman who overheard her plea for more argued that if her children received rice, the children they had left at the camp should also be entitled to rice. The pleas for more grew louder and more insistent. Nabi and the camp leaders failed in their attempts to quiet them.

A few who already had received rice and clothing refused to leave. They had to be pushed out the gate by our guards. A woman who grabbed an extra bucket of rice, ran for the door and was stopped. When the door was opened to let people out, people on the outside pushed back in, many attempting to get more.

Mild mannered, non-confrontational Nabi found himself guarding the gate. He was no match for those pushing to come in. I was of little use. I couldn't understand what was being said and couldn't respond. I certainly couldn't become involved in blocking those who needed to be restrained.

Fortunately, two Afghan policemen patrolling the neighborhood heard the yelling and came to our rescue. Without the assistance of the police someone may have been injured. Nabi and I have never before experienced a distribution that was disorderly nor has Basir. Only after they had gone was there time to reflect on what had happened.

Our first reaction was to punish the camp by telling the leader that we would never help that camp again. However, the truth was the majority of the families were peaceful and very grateful for what they'd received. They understood that whatever rice wasn't distributed to them would go to refugee families living in other camps.

We decided to not punish the many for the actions of a few. In addition, the chaos was created by mothers desperate to feed their families. The more they received the longer they could postpone their family from starving. Should they be punished for refusing to accept no for an answer, given their circumstances? We'll just take better precautions next time.

More Guns and Fear

Yesterday Ashraf Ghani, a presidential candidate, came to our hotel for a press conference. There were men with guns everywhere. For the first time I realized that the more guns there are, the less secure I feel. The hotel with Ashraf Ghani present placed us in what they call a high-value target area. We left the hotel as fast as we could.

Birthing Kits

We met with Dr. Nasrin Oryakhil, Director of the Malalai Maternity Hospital in Kabul. She had recently returned from the United States where she received an International Woman of Courage award from the State Department in a ceremony attended by Michelle Obama. Stop Hunger Now has entrusted us with seven thousand birthing kits to distribute.

The hospital averages eighty deliveries a day: two thousand four hundred a month. If all are given to this hospital, they will be gone in three months.

There were over fifty expectant fathers milling around outside in small groups. When we entered the hospital grounds we became the focus of every man and all conversations stopped. Scanning for friendly faces, I found a few I wanted to approach but a hospital administrator urged us to move quickly inside. Evidently a television crew had recently attempted to do a story about the hospital, and when they began to film the groups of men outside, the camera crew was attacked and driven away.

It is disconcerting to be the center of attention wherever we go. I can't blend into a crowd and neither can Nabi when he is near me. We're "outsiders"—people who extremists plan to drive out of Afghanistan. I have never been yelled at, accosted, threatened or warned during any of my trips to Afghanistan. I am constantly greeted with their right hand placed over their heart by everyone who learns why we are there. We are constantly aware, however, that it only takes one extremist to end our lives and it is impossible to decipher who that person might be.

Upon entering the hospital, we were led to Dr. Oryakhil's office, making certain to not look down any halls on the off chance we would see one of the patients. The nurses had taken the precaution of making certain we wouldn't. Dr. Oryakhil informed us of the desperate need for supplies and equipment, something we've been told by every school and hospital we've visited.

We brought hand-knitted hats, scarves and blankets, donated by volunteers in the United States. I asked Dr. Oryakhil what she would like the knitters to knit, suggesting blankets. She said, "Afghans know about keeping a baby's body warm, and they have blankets. What they don't know is how important it is that babies' heads and feet be kept warm."

Upon leaving the hospital, we were greeted by friendlier faces. Word had spread as to who we were and why we were there but we still didn't take the risk inherent in approaching any of the groups in the yard. I waved to a few and they smiled and waved back. It's unfortunate that we must be this cautious. Meeting with the people is the best part of our trips but it has become something we are increasingly unable to do.

ANOTHER LONG AND REWARDING DAY WITH THE CHILDREN

Today, Nabi and I attended payday for the children sponsored through TIE. It is our favorite event during every trip. We met with as many children as we could. The individual interviews started at 10:00 a.m. in the morning and ended at 3:30 p.m. in the afternoon—no breaks, not even for tea! Below are a few things we learned about sponsored children:

Lailee, age 19, is a starter on the Afghan national women's soccer team. Her team finished 3rd in tournaments held in Kazakhstan against twelve teams and in Norway against fifteen teams. She is one of two sponsored children who are in college. When Nabi jokingly asked whether she would be marrying soon, she laughed and said, "I'll have time for that later."

Neelab, a high school senior, wants to go to college next year but doubts she will. Her parents approve, but her relatives don't. Qudsia explained to me that relatives of some families threaten to ostracize a girl who continues her education beyond what they approve, which can be as minimal as a third grade education.

Nabi offered to speak with her parents. She shrugged and said nothing—resigned to her future. It was a very sad and uncomfortable moment for us all. She never smiled or laughed during the entire interview. We will, of course, support Neelab's college education should she be able to break free. Qudsia will follow up.

Anil passed the national college entrance exam and was disappointed to be told there was no room for him in any of the government's universities. A private university agreed to admit him and reduce his tuition by fifty percent. We reinstated his sponsorship that day. He starts his college education next week. Anil recently won three kickboxing tournaments.

Farida is the beneficiary of our most recent sponsorship. She is ten years old, in 8th grade, and first in her class of fifty students! Eighth grade is not a typo. She is four grades ahead of her peers. Her English is better than every other student we met that day.

She was working on the streets of Kabul with her brother, Haji Gul, until sponsored. Both are so advanced that we are paying the additional cost of them attending a private school. Private schools are much better than public, and students graduating from private schools have a much better chance of getting into college. Private schools charge between $60 and $70 per month.

Farida's mother supports the entire family by washing clothes and baking bread for others. She's not a single mom but as near as we can tell, financially, she effectively is. When we handed her an extra $100, she cupped the palms of her hands and took time to pray.

Saif's kidney problems forced him to drop out of school two years ago. He needs two blood transfusions a week to survive. We were told his family was waiting for his younger brother to be old enough to be his donor. His mother, when asked, said, "I am already losing one son. I don't want to risk losing another." She does not plan to let her younger son donate one of his kidneys. We chose not to ask whether Saif knows.

The lack of confidence in doctors and medicine prevents many children from receiving the medical treatment they need. The financial support we're providing helps keep him alive.

MEDICAL CARE SUPPORT DILEMNA

We are frequently asked to provide financial support for medical care. The requests far exceed what we can provide. The infant mortality rate in Afghanistan is the third highest in the world with one child in four dying before the age of five. The problem with these requests is that no one knows how much or how long medical treatment will be required. They also don't know the full extent of the cost. We are also not in a position to independently evaluate costs and treatment. Nabi, in consultation with Basir and Qudsia has assumed responsibility for determining when to help, an extremely difficult task.

RED VINES—A BIG HIT!

A tub of Red Vines went down well with the sponsored children today. I grabbed a few for myself. The first time I brought Red Vines to Afghanistan, one child tried to write with his. Perhaps I had allowed the licorice to become too hard. The aging of Red Vines is an art much more difficult than aging wine. Licorice can't be too hard or too soft. It must be just right. Wines on the other hand needn't be as precise. They have "character"—a very forgiving concept.

In addition to the tub of licorice I brought, one thousand packages of licorice donated by the American Licorice company will be added to the next shipment to Afghanistan, thanks to Matt Wyse, who made the request.

Female Teachers Need a Ride

In 2005, it was nearly impossible to find a qualified female teacher willing to teach in Lalander, the first village where TIE financed the construction of a school. Many families in the village would not allow their daughters to be taught by a man. We hired Lailuma, a mother who taught classes to girls in her home. She had only had a third grade education herself. She was the most educated woman we could find at the time.

Lailuma, our first female teacher.

This experience made me realize that to maximize enrollment of girls in school, it is important to provide female teachers wherever and whenever possible. During our visit to Farza, we learned that their female teachers were traveling by bus from Kabul at their own expense. After being dropped off on a main road, they still had to walk several miles to where they taught. The combination of no bus schedule and the long walk often made them late and, more importantly, put them at risk. Finding teachers in Kabul willing to make the trip was proving difficult.

A high priority on Farza's wish list this year was providing automobile transportation for these teachers to and from the main road. It is now on the wishes fulfilled list. Solving that problem required paying a taxi driver four dollars a day, less than half the cost of a double latte and blueberry scone!

A Prognosis for Afghanistan

I'm stuck inside the Intercontinental Hotel for the next several hours, making it possible to address the question I'm most often asked: "What will happen when our troops leave?" First, we're not leaving. We're reducing our troop strength from one hundred thousand to less than ten thousand. The three factors that will decide the fate of Afghanistan, in my view are:

1. What happens in Pakistan. Fighting inside Afghanistan will never cease as long as the Taliban are supported, trained and harbored inside Pakistan. The only question is how much territory the Taliban will be able to control.
2. Will the international community provide enough financial support to Afghanistan's central government during the transition period? It cannot presently afford to pay the cost of maintaining the military and police force needed to maintain order in the country and defeat the Taliban.
3. Will the government that replaces President Karzai's gain the support of its people? If it doesn't, they will not defend it and Afghanistan will once again endure an indefinite period of civil war.

John Kerry Breaks an Impasse

With the assistance of the United States government, specifically John Kerry, the recent election was a clear victory for Afghanistan. The two final candidates, Ashraf Ghani and Abdullah Abdullah, with John Kerry's assistance, entered into a shared power agreement before the results of the Afghan election were announced. The winner of the election would not "take all." Power would be shared, not equally, but in ways to be determined. Had they not reached agreement, there was a substantial risk that Afghanistan would have become a failed state.

PRESIDENT ASHRAF GHANI'S FIRST THIRTY DAYS IN OFFICE

Nabi and Ashraf Ghani, the President of Afghanistan, were classmates in the 5th grade and have been friends ever since. They had dinner together at Ashraf's home a year ago, before he decided to run for President. Ashraf has the reputation of being an honest, hard-working man who purposely has stayed away from politics and "insiders." He recently came to office. Within a month he took several actions that made it clear his presidency would be different:

1. He immediately signed a security agreement with the United States, thereby assuring Afghanistan of continued financial and military support.

2. He called for an investigation of Kabul Bank. It has been reported that several shareholders and directors of Kabul Bank acquired shares of stock in the bank by signing promissory notes that have not been repaid. Shareholders have also received large loans from the bank that have also not been paid. The estimated amount of these loans is $900 million. Arrest warrants have been issued for 21 people, including the chief executive officers of the Afghan National Bank and the New Kabul Bank. Both have been accused of fleeing the country to avoid prosecution.

3. He advised the military that there are too many generals and that his approval would be required before adding more. He is

scheduling appointments with existing generals to determine what their roles in the military are.

4. He visited a hospital in Kabul. When told the reception was on the fourth floor, he started with the second. He returned to the hospital unannounced in the very early morning the following day and discovered several of the staff were asleep or absent. Needless to say, that won't happen again.

5. Upon discovering the Presidential kitchen had eighty employees and they were serving the Palace staff thirteen types of Kabob for breakfast, he told the staff they should eat before coming to work. The kitchen staff was reduced by half and Kabob was eliminated from the menu.

6. Upon learning that numerous rich households were not paying their electrical bills, he ordered the Afghan department of Power to collect all outstanding obligations.

As of today, President Ghani has not appointed any ministers. Each one is an "acting minister." The Afghan government has slowed down, which may be a good thing. It will take time to appoint people who will not abuse their office. In addition, while the details of their agreement to cooperate are not known, Ashraf will undoubtedly need to consult with Abdullah Abdullah regarding who should be appointed to each office. By all accounts, the Afghan government needs more than a quick fix. It needs a complete overhaul.

Two of the three factors I believe will have a major impact on Afghanistan's future seem to be on track: a commitment from the United States to continue providing financial support, and a positive change in the central government. The third factor, the impact of the Taliban, has worsened. They have increased their attacks and gained ground in several areas. They have also made it clear that they intend to drive foreigners out by executing several. Nabi and I are keeping as low a profile as possible. We will once again not travel out to the villages this trip.

The good news is pomegranates and grapes are in season. The Afghan grapes are the best I've eaten anywhere in the world. There are so many redeeming qualities about this country. All it needs to prosper is peace.

GIRLS WHO SPEND THEIR PREPUBERTY DAYS AS A BOY

Yesterday we met with Haji Gul and his sister Farida. Their family moved to Kabul because girls aren't being allowed to go to school in their village. Farida's parents want their daughters to be educated. They have six children—two boys and four girls. If you recall, their mother earns most of the money for their family by washing clothes.

I previously wrote about Farida, the ten-year-old who is in the eighth grade (four years ahead of her peers). During the interview we learned Farida spent the first seven years of her life pretending she was a boy. She dressed as a boy and had a boy's haircut.

Her mother explained that Haji Gul wanted a brother, and it was important he have one. They sold gum on the streets as a "team." She went on to explain that it is also safer for a boy to be on the streets than a girl. Sitting on her lap was a young boy. At least that is what we thought. He was, however, a she, pretending to be a boy.

Haji Gul and Farida remained silent throughout their mother's explanation of why Farida was required to be a boy. Neither affirmed or took issue with her explanation. Both were uncomfortable. Nabi and I listened without comment. I asked Farida what happened when children discovered she was a girl. "They made me cry," she responded. She also said she was "very happy" when she was finally allowed to be a girl.

Farida is now happy to be a girl. Her sister has a few years to go as a boy.

Jack Howell suggested that I read the book *The Underground Girls of Kabul*, written by Jenny Nordberg. I brought it with me and began reading it during our sixteen- hour flight from San Francisco to Dubai. It is a very interesting and important book, worthy of everyone's time. In the book there is the following passage:

"If a daughter is born, it is not uncommon for a new mother to leave the delivery room in tears. She will return to the village, her head bowed in shame, where she may be derided by her family and neighbors. She could be beaten and relegated to the outhouse to sleep with the animals for bringing the family another burden. And, if a mother has several daughters already, her husband may be ridiculed as a weakling with whom nature refuses to cooperate.

One kind of child arrives with the promise of ownership and a world waiting outside. The other is born with a single asset, which must be strictly curtailed and controlled: the ability to one day give birth to sons of her own. She, like her mother before her, has arrived in what the United Nations calls the worst place in the world to be born. And, the most dangerous place in which to be a woman." [9]

Qudsia explained to us that it is not uncommon for families in rural villages to raise their daughters as sons. For many, giving birth to a girl is the mother's fault, notwithstanding the fact that male genes determine the sex of a child. In any event, how can anyone assign fault in the birth of a child, regardless of sex? Education is only part of the solution. Eradicating extreme poverty is the other.

This proved to be yet another difficult day. Nabi and I know how important our visits are. However, we both count down the days remaining before we return home. There are now three to go.

WINTER BREAKS NEED NOT BE

Afghan children attend public schools no more than four hours a day, six days a week. Generally, there are two school sessions—one in the morning and the other in the afternoon. Teachers teach only one session. They are therefore free to teach before and after school classes provided the school will allow them to use a room.

For several years, we have been financing before and after school Math, Science, Computer, Native Language and English classes in public schools. We also provide classes in five learning centers built with TIE financing. Villagers help select the subjects taught and the teachers. Currently we employ twenty-three teachers. Collectively they are teaching over one thousand three hundred children with more than fifty per cent being girls. For the past few years we have been loaning computers to government schools to create computer labs. Solving the lack of computers doesn't, however, solve the problem.

Afghan schools are required to teach sixteen subjects to seventh graders and above: Pashto, Farsi, the Koran, Social Skills, Math, Religion, Art, Writing, Behavior, Biology, Chemistry, Physics, English, Physical Education, Science, and Community Service. Geology is added in the tenth grade, bringing the total subjects taught to seventeen.

When computer labs are added, schools must take time away from the other subjects and allocate it to them. In Aqa Ali Shams, a girls' school with six thousand girl students, those fortunate enough to be able to use the labs do so for thirty-five minutes per week. Moreover, two to three students share a computer. The "fortunate ones" don't begin to have enough time.

Afghan schools are closed December, January, and most of February. School administrators are, however, required to work in the buildings during these months and several school are willing to allow us to use school classrooms during this time. Last year we began and will continue providing computer classes every winter that are one and one half hours long and taught six days a week. They provide the classroom and we provide the teacher, wood burning heater, wood, and computers. The total cost per class is less than one thousand dollars per year. The value added is immeasurable.

A major breakthrough occurred in Aqa Ali Shams last year. Parents contributed $4 per child to the winter program. The local shura (governing council) also contributed to the cost of the winter classes. This is the first time there have been any contributions from parents toward classes we've funded.

I take the opportunity, whenever presented, to share with Afghans the fact that it is very common for American parents to contribute to the schools their children attend. In fact, where I live, it's expected. When my children were in school in Lafayette, a local school district sought

$250,000 from parents. It now seeks $1.3 million. We were ecstatic to learn Afghan parents were willing to contribute $4 for winter classes taught to their child! The local *shura* also made a contribution. It may not seem like it to most, but this is a major breakthrough.

AN INEXPENSIVE SUBSTITUTE FOR PAPER

Shortly before I left for Kabul, I had the pleasure of meeting with Julie Krug's class at Walnut Creek Intermediate School. I was able to observe her teaching French and noticed that her students all had white erase boards with dry markers and a cloth. They spelled words and wrote sentences at her command and held them up for her to see. When I took French, I spent a good portion of my time looking out the window and watching the clock. French didn't seem relevant at the time, and is less so now—I should have studied Spanish.

Julie's students were completely engaged. Her energy and passion is clearly infectious. The erase boards made it possible for her to easily determine who was having trouble and what trouble they were having. No one could escape her watchful eye or questioning. Socrates would be proud!

There are light bulb moments in life, and this was one. Erase boards would be a tremendous educational tool in Afghanistan if for no other reason than that every school lacks enough paper and notebooks. Whiteboards can be used over and over again.

After her class Julie told me about a less expensive solution. Buy sheet protectors and insert a yellow sheet of paper inside. That plus a dry marker and piece of cloth would cost less than seventy-five cents per student. Within twenty-four hours I received an email from Julie advising me that a parent, Julie Mendelson, was donating 300 dry erase markers to what had just become another project.

Within a few days, Paul Renaud, who works with Stop Hunger Now, called to ask whether there was something they might provide in addition to rice. "Do they need school supplies?" he asked. Stop Hunger Now donated thousands of sheet protectors, colored paper, and dry erase markers. From conception to execution was less than ten days.

Julie held an after-school stuffing party and brought several of her students to our recent packing party where they inserted sheets of colored paper into one thousand sheet protectors. I was able to pack three hundred fifty sheet protectors and five hundred dry erase markers in my luggage, and they are now being used in several Afghanistan classes. The "teachers and students love them."

Not every project needs to be large or expensive to have a major impact. This one certainly isn't. It also proves what I learned during my first visit in 2005; sharing what we know can be as helpful as sharing what we have.

MORE WELLS

A few months ago, I was contacted by Mahmood Ahmedi. He asked if I knew where wells were needed. Wells provide long term benefits including clean water and shortening the distance women and children must travel to retrieve water for their families. He traveled to Farza, and Basir introduced him to its leaders who in turn convinced him to provide the funds necessary to build two wells. Both have been completed.

Farza's 2013 wish list included playground equipment for the school we'd funded. Done, thanks to Earn It dollars contributed by students attending Corte Madera school in Portola Valley. Can it get any better? American children purchased playground equipment for children living seven thousand miles away, with money they earned.

Three years after receiving a request for support, Farza now has a school for girls, a footbridge that eliminates the risk of drowning for eight hundred children on their way to and from school, two wells, and playground equipment. Equally exciting is the fact that enrollment in the school rose from two hundred fifty girls last fall to three hundred seventy this spring. Build it and they will, in fact, come.

You Can't Be Serious!

On October 8, three days before our packing party, I was informed by email that the Denton program would no longer accept shipments to Afghanistan. The Denton program allows humanitarian aid to be shipped by military aircraft on a space availability basis for free. We've been using that program for years.

We held the packing party anyway. Well over 100 volunteers and supporters brought donations, separated clothing into categories, packed everything into boxes, cut and cleaned Peet's coffee bags for the solar cookers, and made solar cookers and WAPIs. Four days later I flew to Afghanistan knowing that our work might be in vain.

After several weeks, numerous emails and support from several people including Congressman George Miller's office, we were given permission to ship what we had. It's in Germany now waiting for delivery to Kabul. It will arrive in time for the brutal winter months. Had the shipment been disallowed, the following items would still be sitting in the warehouse:

1. Wheelchairs, canes, crutches, and walkers donated by John Muir hospital.
2. Forty-five thousand packages of rice donated by Stop Hunger Now that will provide two hundred seventy-two thousand meals to families living in refugee camps.
3. Two hundred indestructible soccer balls donated by One World Futbol.
4. Three thousand solar cookers made possible by over one hundred high school Interact Clubs, members of District 5170.

5. Fifteen thousand Mylar coffee bags collected from Peet's Coffee stores for the solar cookers.
6. Over two hundred large boxes containing clothing, shoes, school supplies, toys, blankets, stuffed animals, sports equipment and computers.

Every shipment we've made through the Denton program has been significantly larger than the one before. Our first shipment was slightly less than six thousand pounds. This last shipment was sixty-six thousand pounds. We've done very little to promote what we've named as our "Redistribution of Stuff Program." There is only so much stuff my porch can handle and that Jack Howell and I can lift. If promoted, this program could easily be twice as large.

A Very Bad Decision

Removing Afghanistan from the list of countries where humanitarian aid will be transported using the Denton program is a very bad message to send. Essentially our current policy is that planes carrying weapons, military supplies, and equipment necessary to wage war will no longer carry humanitarian aid even though there is room.

US military aid in the region is justified as being in our national security interest. It has been argued repeatedly that we should fight "them" there now rather than be forced to fight "them" here later. The war being fought is a war for hearts and minds.

Hearts and minds are not won with guns, bullets and drones. They are won by providing food, clothing, shelter, education, health care and economic assistance. Providing humanitarian aid is in our national security interest. The Denton program should be reinstated for Afghanistan. (Note: It was reinstated in October 2015 due to "push back." We played a very active role in enlisting Congressmen and others to push back).

A MOTHER, SISTER, FATHER AND WIFE TAKE ON THE TALIBAN
The Taliban recently ambushed a police post in a town bordering Pakistan in the province of Farah. Reza Gul, her husband, daughter and daughter-in-law went to the post to check on her son, a policeman. They discovered her son had been killed. They began fighting the Taliban. Seven hours later they had killed twenty-five Taliban and wounded five more. All four survived. All is not lost in Afghanistan notwithstanding the negative news we're exposed to daily.

CHAPTER 14

Events in 2015
Knitters Astound

❖ ❖ ❖

WHEN WE WERE IN KABUL last April, a maternity hospital director suggested that we ask volunteers to knit hats and socks for babies. Ann Rubin,
working with Afghans for Afghans, sent out the call. The tally is in and
her troops knitted 10,000 pieces, 4,000 of which are hats and socks for
babies. Many of the hats have a note inside from the knitter. They are now
being distributed by the Afshar maternity hospital and TIE's teachers.

Total knits to date: over twenty-five thousand.

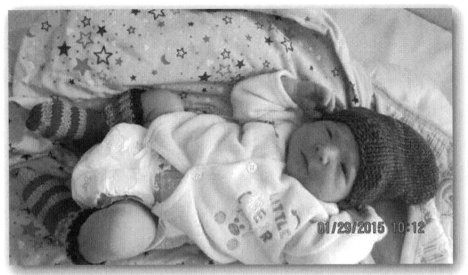

Warm head, warm feet and plenty of room to grow.

It Has Taken More than One Village

We have been extremely fortunate in enlisting people to headline fundraising events, including author, Khaled Hosseini; former Afghan ambassador to the United States, Tayeb Jawad; comedian, Mark Lundholm and magician, Patrick Martin. Our next get together, co-sponsored by SAGE, an Acalanes student organization that can always be counted on for help, will include Tanya Gabrielian, an internationally acclaimed concert pianist. Tanya has performed at Carnegie and Alice Tully Halls in New York, Sydney Opera House, Queen Elizabeth and Wigmore Halls in England, and Salle Cortot in Paris.

I met Tanya last summer at one of her performances in Bigfork, Montana. I stood at the end of a long line of admirers and waited my turn. My first words were, "Would you like to perform in Afghanistan?" Her first were, "Are you serious?" When I responded, "Maybe," she emphatically said, "Yes." That day may hopefully come, but it's not now. It would be too dangerous for her.

She agreed to and did perform at a fundraiser. Nazifa Sidiq and her family once again provided Afghan food prepared by their company, Bolani.

It's thirteen years later and TIE's clock keeps on ticking. Why? Volunteers keep recharging the batteries.

GRADUATION REPORT 2014

The school year ended in December. Eight former "street children" sponsored by TIE graduated from high school, took the national college entrance exam, and are awaiting results. All eight plan to go to college and will likely get in. Information about all eight and our first college graduate was provided by Qudsia at our request:

Zohra, is our first university graduate. Her father died when she was very young so her mother takes in laundry to support her family of seven. Her brothers were able to continue their educations but her older sisters were not. Without sponsorship, Zohra would not have been able to go to school. Zohra's ambition for years has been to be a doctor. She, like most Afghan children I've interviewed, "wants to help her country." She's now a midwife. Zohra's graduation has one further benefit: it moves the country one person closer toward gender equality.

Farhad, entered the sponsorship program in 2000 and he was working on the streets of Kabul to supplement his family's income. He lives with his mother, father, and sisters in a rented two room house. His father sells women's sandals. Farhad is an avid student and has been writing his sponsor in English for three years! He graduated in the top 20% of his class from Amani high school, one of Kabul's top schools. He'd like to visit the United States to personally thank his sponsor. In his most recent letter he wrote, "I used to work on the street before, but since you help me, I can go to school and study and provide for my family and I. Thank you for helping me. I now live comfortably."

Alina lives with her mother and three sisters. They are very, very poor. It is frowned upon to live in a house without a man in Afghanistan so, when her father died, Alina and her family moved in with her uncle. The house has two rooms. Alina sleeps on the floor. Before being sponsored she worked in a nut factory alongside her mother, where she developed severe allergies. Sponsorship made it possible for her to stop working so she could focus on her studies and contribute some groceries for her family.

Despite falling behind in her studies due to health problems, Alina graduated in the top third of her class. She loves biology and like so many others, wants to be a doctor. Fortunately, her mother and uncle both support her continuing her education. Alina wrote recently to her sponsor, "You have helped me improve our family's simple life and brought a smile to our faces during a difficult time. I am happy that, like other kids in the world, I can have a secure future with your help."

Mehdi lives in a two-room house with his parents and five siblings. His father works in a bread shop and does some cleaning. Most of his father's money goes toward rent. Mehdi excelled in English. Like Farhad, he has been writing his sponsor in English for three years. His dream is to go to college and become a pilot so he can "fly everywhere."

Obaidullah's father supports six children on wages earned as a day laborer ($6–8 a day, when there is work). Last year, Obaidullah wrote his sponsor letters in English. In one he wrote, "We have security problem in Afghanistan. Every morning when we wake up we hear bomb blast sound. People can't send their child to school. It is one of my best wishes to get peace in Afghanistan." He also wants to "help the war torn people of Afghanistan so they can have a bright future."

Najeebullah is extremely intelligent, excels at mechanical and electrical engineering and dreams of becoming an engineer. He just graduated from the Kabul Electronics and Mechanics Institution, ranked second in his class. Najeeb wrote, "Whoever goes to school, will know about humanity."

Morsal's father is very old, sick and unable to work. Her mother supports their family of 9 by taking in laundry. Morsal wrote, "Going to school is my happiness. God has never disappointed me; he has always helped me. I have wished that as quickly as possible, that I finish my education in order to help my family and my country...to get rid of the sadness and despair."

Fahim was 7 when his father, a mason, fell off a roof while working and died. His mother, a teacher, did the best she could to raise him but she became very ill and had to retire. Fahim was forced to work on the streets to help support his mother, brother, and sister until he was sponsored in 2010. They all live in one small room and survive on periodic support from his uncles. Four years ago Fahim didn't have a change of clothes.

Fahim graduated from high school, number one in his class. Fahim wrote, "Four years ago I did not have any clothes to wear but today with your help my life is different. I don't feel any different than others."

CHAPTER 15

Advice to Social Entrepreneurs

❖   ❖   ❖

THERE'S ONE SIMPLE MAXIM OF providing aid that is too often overlooked. If you want to know what people need, ask them! Often, aid is provided based upon what organizations decide people need without consulting them.

A soldier in Afghanistan told me about a bridge built over a stream between two Afghan villages. Purportedly, the only thing the two villages have ever done together is destroy the bridge once it was built. Families on both sides of the river were enemies. Villagers were in all likelihood hired to build the bridge and were happy to receive the income. The bridge itself, however, was something they didn't want or need.

When visiting Afghanistan, we receive many funding requests. Our practice is to not act upon any requests until all have been received. Two English words we can take credit for teaching Afghans are "wish" and "list." Every funding request goes on a "wish list."

When the wish-list process was first implemented, something unexpected happened. Every funding request had to be accompanied with an itemized budget. People were told to list labor costs separately from materials. We have not received one proposal that included a request to pay for labor, except on a few occasions when technical skills were required and a volunteer could not be found to do the work.

It is possible that villages realize they are competing for TIE's wish-list funds and therefore haven't included labor in their budgets. I think it's more than that. Every village we have assisted has a very strong and highly developed sense of community and a willingness to work together to achieve common goals. The five-classroom school for girls in Farza, two bridges, two irrigation projects, three learning centers, and several other smaller projects requiring labor were built entirely by Afghan volunteers.

Once the wish lists are all in, the decision-making process begins. First, we consider the nature of the impact and the number of people benefited. Requests we haven't approved include an irrigation project and the expansion of a road used by automobiles. The first benefitted only three families. Expanding the road helped people who could afford to own a car, which is not our target group. We're focused on the bottom rungs of the economic ladder. In both cases, we explained our decision, and we haven't had similar requests since.

The wish-list process is the best way to allocate time and dollars and it has transformed our relationship with Afghan villages. TIE was once an outside temporary benefactor, but has become a long-term partner. The projects are as much, if not more, theirs than ours.

One dilemma we often face is whether to consult with village leaders and government officials in an area before proceeding with projects proposed by villagers. If these people are not consulted, it's an affront to their authority and power. They may then oppose a project and make it more difficult to complete. If consulted, they may expect *baksheesh* (a bribe).

We believe the building of the school in Farza was delayed because we refused to pay an official his requested one thousand dollars. We waited for the villagers to challenge and overcome his delaying tactics. Ultimately, he couldn't stop them or the project. Several others have been less direct. They mention what they want in passing, such as a camera, computer, or phone, fully expecting that we will buy these for them.

Everyone accuses others of corruption, apparently not recognizing that expecting or receiving gifts for what their position already requires them to do is corrupt.

If we opened our door to *baksheesh*, the line outside would be very long. In Farza, we purposely stayed out of the local politics and worked directly with the Ministry of Education in Kabul. Whatever opposition or delays there were inside Farza were resolved by the villagers or the Ministry.

We have been very successful in working directly with villagers and have avoided dealing directly with officials expecting a gift. Whenever possible we make going through channels their responsibility not ours. When they run into a wall, we move up the chain of command.

CHAPTER 16

Earn It

❖   ❖   ❖

WHEN WE FIRST BEGAN PARTICIPATING in school fundraising efforts, I had heard about "Pennies for Peace" drives conducted by the Central Asia Institute. It doesn't take too long to calculate that ten thousand pennies equals a hundred dollars. Try lugging tens of thousands of pennies into the bank, or better yet, roll them into fifty-cent rolls. I chose the phrase "Change for Change," subliminally suggesting they include, nickels, dimes, and quarters.

A few years and "Change for Change" drives later, it became evident that, notwithstanding how inspired students were during assemblies, most were simply asking their parents and others for change. What they collected went into the change jars located in their classrooms, and that was the extent of their commitment—not a big deal except to the students who had earned what they contributed.

I then adopted the slogan, "The buck stops here." The saying afforded me an opportunity to provide a brief history lesson on Harry Truman, explain the meaning of double entendre, and urge students to accept personal responsibility for helping others.

The slogan worked. Soon after the first drive began, I received an e-mail from a mother explaining how her daughter, Sophie Hall, had been so inspired by what she'd heard and seen that she'd insisted on making and selling baked goods with a friend that weekend. They earned eighty-seven dollars in two days. Sophie, her friend, and her mother were thrilled.

Encouraged by the impact the "buck stops here" slogan was having on students, I raised the bar. I began telling students they were not allowed to ask for money from their parents. When I said that not one penny could come from their parents, one young boy stood and asked, "Can I use my allowance?"

I asked, "Do you earn it?" He lowered and then shrugged his shoulders disappointed to learn that his unearned allowance didn't qualify.

I later introduced the parent-disqualification rule to Corte Madera elementary school in Portola Valley. Portola Valley is a very affluent community in Silicon Valley. I ruled out parents as a source for student donations, not knowing what impact it would have on fundraising. Truth is, I didn't and don't care how much is raised. It's more important that students take personal responsibility and earn what they contribute. Fundraising drives are not about raising money: they are part of raising children.

Three months after the first Earn It drive began in Corte Madera, I was invited back to report on my most recent trip to Afghanistan. At the end of my talk, three students came to the front of the room. One proudly announced, "Mr. MacKenzie, when you came here last time, you said we couldn't go to our parents for money." She went on to explain how they had earned money.

One student had taught others how to play lacrosse for a small fee. His mother e-mailed me video clips of his lessons. Others had prepared and served food at dinner parties they held, played an instrument in public, baked and sold bakery goods, walked dogs, mowed lawns, washed cars, and earned money babysitting. Several parents had helped their children make signs, set up tables and booths, and taught their children how to bake. I have had only positive feedback from parents regarding Earn It campaigns.

CORTE MADERA PORTOLA VALLEY

Corte Madera supports four Afghan street children. The first Earn It year, students did the math. They each needed to earn thirty-two dollars to reach the amount required to support all four children that year. They presented me with a check for $2,512.57. This was $512.57 more than needed and more than twice what had been collected during previous drives.

I was told I could use the additional money for whatever I thought best. I raised the income of "their" street children from forty to fifty dollars per month. Children on both sides of the world were ecstatic.

The next year, Corte Madera students presented me with a check in an amount over four thousand five hundred dollars. The extra money was used to purchase desks for the girls' school built in Farza. During a presentation at Corte Madera, I was able to show photos of Afghan children sitting at "their" desks. Hundreds of Afghans now know that American children are earning money to help them.

I've received several Earn It stories—two of which are my favorites. A Corte Madera student informed his teacher that his mother had asked if she could just write a check for fifty dollars. He told his teacher, "Don't worry, I took care of it." He had explained to his mother why he needed and wanted to take personal responsibility for "his" donation.

Another Corte Madera student earned and saved a hundred dollars over a one-year period. He had a hundred-dollar bill in his wallet that he lost on his way to school. His wallet was found, but the bill was gone. Upon learning of his loss, members of the community stepped forward and contributed to replace what he'd lost. What's unique and very encouraging about this story is that he had earned this money between the first and second drives. He had accepted personal responsibility for helping Afghan children throughout the year, not just during a fundraising drive.

PRIZES AND COMPETITION DILUTE THE MESSAGE

We considered and decided to not introduce competition into our fund-raising drives ourselves. Competition and awards would likely bring in more money, but it would, we believe, undermine what we are striving to achieve—students developing their own sense of responsibility and concern for the welfare of others. Raising children with the values we would like to impart is more important than raising money.

Jacob van Styn and his family get it!

The Earn It approach to fundraising has been, in our experience, a winner. Students establish personal goals, often work in groups, devise and execute plans of action, and experience the joy and pride of having personally made a difference. At the receiving end, children who must work to survive know that children who needn't work are doing so to make their lives easier.

STANDING BY THE JAR

Parenthetically, I've worked alongside and counted TIE donation jars for years. I've watched people thumb through fives, tens, and twenties to extract one-dollar bills. Many dig deep to find change. I've been tempted to launch a campaign with the slogan, "Keep your change…they need dollars." Laying on the guilt is probably not a good idea, however. If you want to make a difference in the lives of volunteers standing next to a donation jar, throw in a twenty. You will help make their day—and yours.

CHAPTER 17

Diamonds in the Rough

❖　❖　❖

ASK ANY SMALL NONGOVERNMENTAL ORGANIZATION (NGO), and it will tell you how frustrated it is with the United States Agency for International Development (USAID), our government's foreign-aid agency. USAID has no program to fund smaller NGOs—at least none we have been able to discover. US foreign aid is delivered either by government agencies, the State Department, the military, or large organizations in the business of providing aid.

Every USAID employee I've met recognizes the value of smaller NGOs and wants the authority to fund organizations like TIE. Administrators within USAID have explained that they don't have enough personnel to make small grants. "It takes just as long to process a one hundred-thousand-dollar grant as a million-dollar grant, and we don't have time or people to do both," is the explanation. One year, a USAID administrator in Afghanistan informed me that the smallest grant USAID had approved that year was five hundred thousand dollars and that it was "an exception." Every other grant was over a million dollars.

In 1971, a classmate friend, John Chalik, and I started a cheese-and-wine store in Berkeley named Curds and Whey. Bankers told us the same thing: the loan we'd need wasn't worth their time. Banks competed for large accounts and loans. Several years later, perhaps decades (what baby boomer can keep track of the passage of time?), banks began aggressively competing for small-business accounts. The banking industry woke up to the fact that the failure rate of small-business loans was lower, yields from them were higher, and successful small businesses become larger customers over time.

USAID is making the same mistake that banks made years ago by turning away small nonprofits at the door. The advantages of small over large are significant:

- They are able to enlist passionate, committed volunteers who work for free. Therefore, their cost of projects, programs, and operations are considerably lower. Donor dollars go much further with smaller nonprofits.
- They are capable of making decisions quickly and adjust faster to changed circumstances.
- If they make a mistake, they lose small.
- They are not buried in studies and useless reports.

THE HIDDEN COST OF NOT COMING BACK

During my second visit to Lalander, Malik Weiss, a village leader I've mentioned before, reached into his back pocket, pulled out a two-inch stack of soiled business cards, and handed them to me. I recognized the names of several large aid organizations. While thumbing through the cards, he said, "All of those people came to my home and never came back. I thought you would be one of those people."

The failure to return does more than disappoint. Having had that many aid workers visit his home, eat his food, enjoy his hospitality, and "never come back," he now views foreign aid as just another business, doing more for the wealthy than the poor. He is not alone in this perception.

CORRUPTION IN THE HUNDREDS OF MILLIONS

Nabi and I met with an Afghan government minister whose name I won't reveal. I am certain he would not want his comment on the record. I shared with him the perception of Afghans and Americans that there was too much corruption in the Afghan government. Couldn't they do more to combat corruption? I asked.

His response was telling. He told us, "The total amount of aid countries has publicly claimed they've provided Afghanistan is thirty billion dollars. We [the Afghan government] have seen eight billion. Where's the other twenty-two?"

The US government has admitted on more than one occasion that it has been unable to account for hundreds of millions of dollars spent in Afghanistan. Smaller organizations track every dollar they spend; they are called upon to do so by their donors.

LACK OF AUTHORITY

The lack of authority to commit funds was extremely frustrating to American soldiers who fought in Afghanistan, charged with the responsibility of gaining the support of "the locals." Providing financial support to villages is essential in obtaining good intel and in the war for hearts and minds.

An American mother asked me to contact her son while I was in Kabul in 2011. He was responsible for establishing and improving relationships in several villages near Kandahar. That area had one of the highest concentrations of Taliban.

"How am I supposed to develop relationships?" he asked. "I have no authority to spend anything without first submitting a report and getting prior approval. Approval takes at least three months." He also didn't have the benefit of a briefing by the soldier he was replacing. Their assignments didn't overlap.

By the time this young soldier could identify which villagers he should meet, determine whom to trust, learn what they needed, write a report, get approval, and obtain funding, his tour of duty could easily have been over. If his replacement's tour of duty didn't overlap with his and there was no record of what had been done or promised while he was there, the process would start all over again.

A year later at a restaurant in Washington DC, I overheard a soldier at the adjoining table discussing his tour of duty in Afghanistan. I leaned and pulled my chair closer until it was embarrassingly obvious that I was eavesdropping. He invited me to his table, and we spoke for over an hour. I haven't had many opportunities to speak with soldiers who have fought in Afghanistan; our paths seldom cross.

He was a marine company commander who'd fought in the "tribal area" near the Pakistan border. The tribal areas are where the heaviest fighting occurs. He reminded me of my lean, mean, fighting-machine days that ended at the conclusion of my army basic training in Fort Benning, Georgia, in 1970.

I told the soldier about the conversation I'd had with the soldier in Kandahar. He responded, "I had authority to call in airstrikes, fire mortar rounds, and initiate a ground attack that would cost lives and hundreds of thousands of dollars. Yet I couldn't spend a dime to build a well in a village without permission which took several months to get." His limit for a single project was five thousand dollars.

TURNOVER

Leaving aside the issue of size, the high personnel turnover rate in USAID and the State Department in Afghanistan has had a severe negative impact on their performance. Every time I visited USAID or the State Department in Afghanistan, I encountered significant personnel changes within both. Whomever I spoke with had either just arrived or would be leaving soon. People on their way out told us we needed to wait until their replacements arrived. Replacements told us they were new and needed time before they could respond. Not one could give us a straight answer or act without going through an extensive, time-consuming vetting process. Within a few years, I concluded that going to their offices wasn't worth our time or the risk.

SHUTTING OUT SOCIAL ENTREPRENEURS

The United States' foreign aid is contracted out by Washington to large aid providers. How's that going? The prevailing view among people I know is that our foreign aid is bureaucratic, wasteful, corrupt, and too often ineffective. Organizations seeking funding from "Washington" were described to me by one congressman as "beltway bandits." By supporting smaller grassroots projects and programs, USAID and the State Department would be able to improve their image with the millions of American volunteers who now have no faith in the beltway.

USAID should provide a small budget, desks, phones, file cabinets, and assistants to two motivated, can-do problem solvers authorized to fund small, nonprofit organizations for three years. Why two administrators? One would award grants to successful small nonprofits without requiring extensive studies and reports, and the other would impose the same conditions required of large grants today.

Audits and unannounced site visits would be required. I'm absolutely certain after three years the case would be proven. Small businesses proved their case with banks. Small nonprofit organizations will do the same.

CHAPTER 18

The Solution to Access

MASOOD SATARI, AN AFGHAN LIVING in the Bay Area of California, contacted me several years ago. He was frustrated by his inability to mobilize his friends and others to translate Khan Academy videos. Through Masood I learned that Salman Khan, founder of Khan Academy, had stumbled onto an extraordinary vision while tutoring his cousin: educate the world by providing educational videos online for free. Masood wanted Trust in Education to take on the challenge of translating Khan videos into Dari and Pashto, Afghanistan's main and official languages.

The idea sat in the pile of good ideas until Gerard Van Styn stepped up in the Spring of 2014 to spearhead the effort. To say it hasn't been easy is a gross understatement. Nevertheless, two years later we have translated all of the one thousand Khan Academy Math videos into Dari and are working on translating them into Pashto.

OFFLINE LEARNING
Educational videos available online are great for children with computers and access to the Internet. The vast majority of Afghan children have neither. When Nabi and I asked the assistant to the Minister of Education in 2014 whether the government could provide Internet access in the three

schools where we'd provided computers, he smiled and said, "We don't have enough money to provide books in all our schools."

In response to the lack of access to videos online, we've implemented a plan to make them available offline. First, we will make whatever we produce available to anyone for free, provided they agree to do the same. Next, we are establishing computer libraries in schools and in libraries where students can study on their own. Currently there are six with an average utilization rate of over five hundred students a day. Finally, Gerard made a convincing argument that tablets, not desktop computers, are the future. We're purchasing tablets, loading them with the videos, and letting children check them out as they would books. Tablets make it possible to bring education into all homes, including those where children are not able or allowed to go to school.

WILL THEY USE THEM?

During our spring visit to Kabul in 2015, Nabi and I showed two school principals one of the translated math videos. The first laughed and said, "This is better than a teacher. Afghan teachers don't like to repeat themselves." The beauty of educational videos is that students can rewind, stop, and replay a video until they understand. They are not forced to move on to the next lesson before they are ready, or be held back by other students. They can learn on their own time and at their own pace.

The second principal said, "We have teachers in this school whose only qualification is that they knew somebody or are someone's relative." The lack of qualified teachers, particularly female teachers, is a problem. The "brain drain" that occurred during the reign of the Taliban continues to have a major impact on education. The videos make it possible for Afghan students to learn beyond the limits of their teachers. We know Afghan teachers are also watching them online.

What's Next?

When deciding what subject to translate next, I learned that one of our sponsored children who graduated from college, was not able to work at a bank because they only hired Afghans who could speak and understand English. There was the answer. English is the money language. In developing countries, whoever is proficient in English will have more job opportunities and likely earn more money.

I called a friend who taught English as a second language (ESL) and learned that English is taught in English. There is no need to translate ESL lessons! This was going to be easy. We'd just download all the ESL lessons off the internet and take them to Afghanistan on flash drives.

It didn't take long to discover there are ESL lessons on the internet but they aren't free. Why would they be? Who can afford to spend all the time and money necessary to make ESL videos and make them available for free? How could we?

Funding projects is always a challenge and we found a solution, children. American children are now making ESL videos that we are editing, posting on YouTube and making available offline in Afghanistan. Our children will help children all over the world learn a language that may increase their employment opportunities and income.

How Important Could This Become?

Along with Khan Academy, we are making education accessible for free. Students are able to learn on their own time and at their own pace. They will no longer be limited to learning what their teachers know. Finally, educational videos will last as long as homo sapiens do, without further funding. This is extremely important given how challenging it is to raise funds year after year. Salman Khan has opened the floodgate to education. We just need to make thousands of videos. Help us. It is likely to be the most valuable contribution to education that we will make.

One of six computer libraries with a current utilization
rate of over five hundred students a day!

CHAPTER 19

Gender Equality—
the Lack Thereof

❖ ❖ ❖

THE MOST FRUSTRATING, DISTURBING, AND important challenge in Afghanistan is changing the self-serving views held by domineering men that impact the roles and rights of Afghan women. The perception of women as subservient to and less valuable than men is not exclusively a "male thing." However, men, due to their relative size and strength, are able to enforce whatever laws and customs they choose.

In Afghanistan, women have been and will continue to be forced to marry men without their consent, bartered away to resolve disputes between families, sold, raped with impunity, and killed or imprisoned for refusing to enter into a forced marriage or running away from an abusive one. All of these actions against women are illegal in Afghanistan. The enforcement of laws there is, however, anything but assured.

We have all read about horrific incidents, trusting that they were isolated and few, a reflection of the media's propensity to report the extreme. However, after conducting a survey in 2010, UN researchers found the truth is that "such practices are pervasive, occurring in varying degrees in all communities, urban and rural, and among all ethnic groups."

Below are portions taken from the United Nations report:

1. "Forced marriage is not a harmful tradition in our culture. I know my daughter's best interests and since she does not leave the house, she does not understand the world, and it will not be possible or acceptable for her to choose her own husband. She has no right to select her own husband, and I am in the best position to choose for her." (Interview with a male member of Faryab Provincial Council, April 2010)
2. In January 2009, a 20-year-old woman sought protection from a court to avoid being forced to marry a man chosen for her when she was four years old. As the court session was about to start, a group of 300 people, who supported the forced marriage, attacked the district complex, abducted the girl, and forcibly took her to her in-laws' house. All efforts to contact the woman by the United Nations failed, and her whereabouts are unknown.
3. The police and judiciary often fail to enforce laws that respect women's rights and take a selective rather than impartial approach to administering justice. They often pursue cases where women are perceived to have transgressed social norms and fail to act when women report violence and in cases of child marriages, claiming these are private matters. In many instances judicial officials have tended to punish female victims of violence rather than its perpetrators.
4. Girls given in *baad* [exchanging a girl to resolve a dispute between families] are often treated like slaves...they endure mistreatment, physical violence, and humiliation as retaliation for the crime committed by the male family member...Insults and beatings are common, and, in some cases, the family denies the girl all contact with her parents and siblings.

5. 57 % of Afghan marriages are child marriages, where one partner is under the age of 16. In a study of 200 married girls, 40% had been married between the ages of 10 and 13, 32.5% at 14, and 27.5 % at the age of 15.

6. Often, if a widow does not remarry into the same family, she risks losing her children. According to Afghanistan's Civil Code, once children have reached a certain age (nine for girls, seven for boys) guardianship goes to the father, or in the case of death or divorce, to the family of the father.

7. So-called honor killings recognize a man's right to kill a woman with impunity because of the damage that her immoral actions have caused to family honor...The perceived dishonor is often the woman's flight from a forced marriage, choosing her own marriage partner, or engaging in questionable conduct with a member of the opposite sex. Article 398 of Afghanistan's Penal Code reduces punishment for killings perpetuated in the name of 'honor.' A man guilty of an honor killing is therefore legally entitled to special consideration that could result in reducing his punishment.

8. Girls who marry as children almost never continue with their education. Young brides take on heavy domestic chores, new restrictions on their mobility, and social norms that view marriage and schooling as incompatible. Pressure comes from many directions, including the families of other students, who do not want their daughters attending school with married girls." [10]

Government Support for Male Supremacy

In March 2012, the Ulema Council, a government-appointed and financially supported body of 150 "leading Muslim clerics," legitimized the inferiority of women. The Council issued a code of conduct that included a statement that "Men are fundamental and women are secondary." It further determined that "women should avoid mingling with strange men in various social activities such as education, in bazaars, in offices and other aspects of life." The Council urged the government to require women to wear the veil and forbid them from mixing with men in the workplace or traveling without a male chaperone. Within four days after it was issued, the Council's code of conduct was approved by President Karzai.

Not only is there support for male supremacy by the uneducated, there is reinforcement of that view from the top religious leaders in the country and former President Karzai. Little wonder that Save the Children concluded in 2011 that Afghanistan was the worst place in the world to be a woman.

CHAPTER 20

Shelters for Women

❖ ❖ ❖

IN OCTOBER 2012, THE WORLD was deeply saddened and outraged to learn of the shooting of Malala Yousafzai, aged fourteen, who was shot by a Taliban gunman while riding home on a school bus in Pakistan. A planned assassination attempt on her occurred simply because she publicly advocated that girls be allowed to attend school. She survived and lives, knowing that members of the Taliban have vowed to kill her and her father. She is now a recipient of a Nobel Peace Prize for her unwavering and fearless advocacy of women's rights.

Shelters for women who have fled their homes have been established in Afghanistan. Afghan legislators and religious leaders have called for the closing of the shelters, accusing them of being houses of prostitution. Most Americans don't realize how grave the consequences can be to an Afghan woman who flees from an abusive husband, refuses to accept an arranged marriage, or rebels against a subservient life prescribed by her parents, more often than not by her father.

I learned about the women's shelters through Jill Humphries. She conducted several filmed interviews inside one shelter in Kabul that we have been able to help. This led to the production of an online video narrated by Dan Rather, *Spirit Indestructible*, released in 2013. It can still be viewed on YouTube. Jill shared with me the story of Zakia, one of the women living in the shelter.

Zakia was sold to a much older man by her father, a Talib. Her husband already had two wives and over ten children when Zakia arrived. She was abused by the entire family, most severely by her husband. One day, Zakia ran away and returned to her family home for shelter. Zakia's husband called Zakia's mother and threatened to kill one of Zakia's brothers if they did not kill Zakia.

Zakia's mother then called her father, who was in Pakistan. He and one of her brothers came home. They took Zakia for a walk after dinner. When they were deep inside a graveyard, they slashed her sixteen times—twice across her throat, once from above the sternum to below her navel, exposing her intestines. Zakia managed to walk to the street, holding her neck, and asked two Afghan men for help. They did not want to get involved and called the police. Zakia's father has told her that if she ever leaves the shelter, he will find and kill her.

CHAPTER 21

Does Size Matter?

❖   ❖   ❖

NABI TAWAKALI, A FRIEND AND traveling companion when I visit Afghanistan, and I had a conversation with a highly regarded village leader bearing on the subject of women's rights. The leader had been chosen to be part of a team to negotiate with the Taliban to end the fighting. Through Nabi, I said, "I am concerned about negotiations with the Taliban. There won't be any women in the room when you are negotiating."

After a very lengthy response, he concluded by saying, "Doesn't Budd know that women's brains are smaller than men's?" I didn't know how to respond. Were women's brains smaller? Surely, the relative sizes of brains couldn't possibly justify the subordination of women. In anger, albeit disguised, I asked Nabi to "Tell him it's not the size of the brain that counts, it's how much of the brain someone is using." Two Afghan employees, listening to the conversation, understood what I'd said and smiled. Nabi, my cultural-sensitivity monitor, looked at me and said, "I think we should change the subject." We did, and he was right.

Upon returning home, I sought to disprove the foundation of his male-supremacy argument, thinking that a Google search would prove him wrong. It didn't. Women's brains are, in fact, on average, ten percent smaller than men's. There are, however, no studies I could find establishing a correlation between brain size and intelligence. In fact, there's evidence supporting the opposite.

When I attended law school in the late sixties, fewer than fifteen percent of the students in my first year class were women. Currently, over fifty percent of entrants to law, business, medical schools, and colleges are women. Rumor, from an unknown "reliable" source, has it that many small college admissions offices are keeping the ratio of women on campus below sixty percent. Apparently, if a college has more than sixty percent women on campus, neither men nor women want to enroll. As a consequence, male applicants have a seven percent better chance of being accepted to these colleges than female candidates. Affirmative action and reverse discrimination favoring men? Who would have thunk it would happen?

Even if science were able to establish that there is no correlation between brain size and intelligence, it won't change anyone's mind who believes "a woman's place is in the home" and "a man is king of his castle." I haven't heard the phrase, "barefoot, pregnant, and in the kitchen" since the late sixties, when Gloria Steinem championed women's rights. No one in this country dared then, or dares now, to advocate anything less than equal rights for women.

Women's Rights Within and Outside our Borders

Three gender equality causes remaining in the United States today are the "glass ceiling," equal pay, and control over reproductive rights. The ceiling has been cracked, will be broken and shattered over time. Pay for men and women will eventually equalize. Control over reproductive rights was settled by the United States Supreme Court in 1973 in the case of Roe v. Wade (1973), but remains a contentious issue. In Afghanistan and elsewhere, women struggle for the right just to get out of the house, go to school, work, and marry when and whomever they choose. We must not allow that to continue.

Periodically, I encounter the argument, "We shouldn't interfere with their culture." It's one explanation given for not becoming involved in the struggle for women's rights outside the United States—and one with which I couldn't disagree more. The oppression of women, like genocide, should not be classified as a protected cultural difference. Comparing oppression to genocide seems excessive, even to me. But oppression, the lifelong killing of and control over the human spirit, is no less inhumane. Insofar as human rights are concerned, the world is flat and there are no borders that shouldn't be crossed to protect them.

CHAPTER 22

Hope Is Not a Strategy

❖ ❖ ❖

As HORRIFIC AS THE INJUSTICES inflicted on women are, it's equally troubling to realize how little is done to protect them. The United States government and Trust in Education, for that matter are engaged in what is essentially a "hope strategy" for women. We educate, advocate, and commiserate, hoping that women will become "empowered," acquire more rights over time, and that things will get better.

We support education of women, provide medical care, make microcredit loans, host conferences, sponsor student-exchange programs and provide a myriad of other types of aid, all in an effort to improve women's lives. Yet, women are being sold, traded, married, and engaged without their consent. They are imprisoned, beaten, and killed for failing to live lives prescribed by their fathers. We are skirting around the edges of women's lives, ignoring what is most important to them: that they be free of male domination, oppression, and abuse. What can we do?

First, the United States government should announce publicly to the world that Americans care about women, women's rights, and gender equality! The achievement of gender equality should become a national priority, as important to us as oil, commerce, and defense. Next, government agencies providing foreign aid must be required to consider whether countries are moving toward gender equality or not in awarding grants.

The projects and programs of countries that are moving toward gender equality should have a better chance of being funded

We would not be forcing a government to do anything. The choice would be theirs. The money they receive is "ours," and we can spend it wherever we decide. It is time we put our money where our values lie.

PETITION TO THE UNITED STATES GOVERNMENT

Below is a petition to the United States government we've asked people to support:

"The undersigned believe gender equality is an inalienable right that all civil societies should support, including those receiving American foreign aid. To that end, we propose:

That United States foreign policy recognize and include the promotion and attainment of gender equality as one of its top priorities.

That in the allocation of foreign aid, the United States government be required to take into consideration the extent to which a country has laws and regulations, or has taken actions that, promote or adversely impact the achievement of gender equality."

I learned early on through my visits to Afghanistan the truism that "money talks louder than words," particularly in countries dependent upon foreign aid. It's time we took full advantage of the power of the dollar.

Julianne Moore, Oscar recipient for Best Actress in 2015 and Tony award winner, Alan Cumming, have both endorsed this petition. It will take tens of thousands more endorsers before politicians weigh in. If you wish to endorse the petition, send us an e-mail: trustineducation@gmail.com. Whoever has political influence, use it. This is one request of government that won't cost us anything

We can impact their future.

CHAPTER 23

Call to Arms

MY AWAKENING HAS NOT BEEN without costs. I have become committed to addressing needs and problems that far surpass our capacity to help, let alone resolve. Having spent most of my life facing and solving finite problems, I occasionally find this never-ending work overwhelming and depressing. Nabi and I have encountered more tragedies and injustices in a year than most will over a lifetime. Misfortune and good fortune are not distributed equally—Life is not fair.

Working in the trenches with the poorest among us can be isolating. It becomes increasingly difficult to relate to conversations with those who are unfamiliar and worse, uninterested—particularly people whose interest in what aid workers prefer to discuss is polite but passing at best. Tuning the other out is common to both.

Humanitarian aid workers know exactly what I mean. When they return from an assignment, they no longer relate as well to the life and people they left behind. Often they are more comfortable living in environments and communities that most would consider intolerable and dangerous. Why? Because there is more goodwill among men and women and they are able to make a meaningful difference in the lives of others.

The greatest disappointment in taking up the challenge comes from discovering how many people aren't concerned about the welfare of others—that is, beyond immediate family, community and friends. Shouldn't the affluent be engaged in leveling the field for the ill-fated? Everyone recognizes that misfortune and good fortune are not distributed equally.

Once I was advised by a friend to "avoid using the word *should* because everyone is entitled to his or her own conscience, beliefs and values." Leaving aside the teaching of all religions, this may be true, but what I once argued was a moral imperative need not be—Ignore *should*.

My primary motivation in writing this book has been to encourage and ideally inspire others to get off their couch just as I did after reading the article in Parade magazine. The most important lesson I learned as a result is that the personal satisfaction derived from helping others is far greater than any other reward. This has turned out to be the most difficult, tiring, and frustrating work I have every done. It is also by far the most rewarding.

After having observed human behavior for over seventy years, it dawned on me several years ago, that givers lead happier, more fulfilling lives and are more enjoyable to be around. My only regret is that I didn't make these discoveries earlier in life. Consequently, I devote a considerable amount of time sharing these revelations with children of all ages.

WC Fields provided another reason for engaging in the war on poverty. Just before his death, a friend visited his hospital room and was surprised to see him thumbing through a Bible. When asked what he was doing with a Bible, Fields replied, "I'm looking for loopholes."

Whatever the motivation, get off the couch and devote more of your life to helping others. It's likely to be a "loophole."

1 Shakespeare, W. (1623) *As You Like It*. London: First Folio

2 "Les Révélations d'un Conseilleur de Carter: Oui, la CIA est Entrée en Afghanistan avant les Russes..." *Le Nouvel Observateur* [Paris], January 15-21, 1998, p.76.

3 Chandrasekaren, R, (2011) In Afghanistan, U.S. shifts strategy on women's rights as it eyes wider priorities. The*iii Washington Post*, 14 March 2011, p.23-25.

4 Sharifi, U, (2011) Big, fat Afghan weddings facing government ban. *China Daily*, 4 September 2011. P.6.

5 Save the Children (2011) v *The 2011 Mothers' Index*, New York: Save the Children.

6 http://www.state.gov (2010) *Remarks on Global Alliance for Clean Cookstoves at the Clinton Global Initiative.* [ONLINE] Available at: http://www.state.gov/secretary/20092013clinton/rm/2010/09/147500.htm. [Accessed 6 October 2016].

7 Kipling, R, (1910) *If.* 1st ed. New York: Doubleday, Page & Company.

8 Marzban, O, (2012) Afghan Olympian Has Eye On Prize -- Equality For Women. *Radio Free Europe/Radio Liberty*, 2 August 2012.

9 Nordberg, J, (2014) *The Undergroundix Girls of Kabul.* 1st ed. New York: Random House

10 United Nations (2010) *Harmful Traditional Practices and Implementation of the Law on Elimination of Violence against Women in Afghanistan*, Kabul; Geneva: UNAMA.

About the Author

❖   ❖   ❖

AFTER GRADUATING FROM AMHERST COLLEGE in 1967, Budd moved westward to Boalt Law School and Haas Business School, UC Berkeley, where he graduated with a joint JD/MBA degree. This particular educational experience included observing violent marches on and off campus and suffering the effects of tear gas released by members of the National guard who were called to monitor the demonstrations and prevent the destruction of property. The Vietnam War and its fallout impacted every member of his generation, most of whom vowed to "give peace a chance."

Thirty-six years later, the United States was engaged in two wars, one in Iraq and the other in Afghanistan. Reflecting on the Vietnam war era, Budd realized that being anti-war as a student was easy. Protestors made a few signs, appeared at rallies, signed petitions, wrote letters, disrupted classes and traffic. What was noticeably absent was a concern for the victims of war.

Budd began in 2003 by raising the funds necessary to build a school in Afghanistan, intending to do no more. Then he "made the mistake of becoming informed," by visiting Afghanistan when the school opened in 2005 and reading *Charlie Wilson's War*. He saw first hand the conditions and impact of the war we had supported against the Russian occupation of Afghanistan.

While visiting Afghanistan, he realized building one school was not enough. Trust in Education, a nonprofit 501(c)(3) organization was formed and the rest is history, the most stressful, challenging, frustrating, and rewarding period of his life.

Thirteen years and twenty visits to Afghanistan later, it's time to share what he's observed with others. Countless well-attended speaking engagements and supporters convinced him to "put it down in writing." Ergo this book. He guarantees that every reader will learn several things they didn't know.

Budd has received numerous public recognitions for his community service, including;

- Recognized by His Holiness the Dalai Lama in 2014 when Budd was awarded the "Unsung Heroes of Compassion" honor along with fifty other men and women from around the globe.
- Chosen as the "Citizen of the Year" by the City of Lafayette (2004)
- Admitted as an honorary member and received a Paul Harris Fellow award from a Lafayette rotary Club.
- Awarded the Stu Stauffer Friends of Education Award by Acalanes High School (2004)
- Received a Humanitarian Award in Contra Costa County (2012)
- Awarded a Peace and Justice Award by the Mt. Diablo Peace and Justice Center (2010)

Budd lives in Lafayette, California, allocating his time between serving as Trust in Education's lead volunteer, doing what remains on his "bucket list," playing pickleball, and as one third grader described it, "being a world saver." He spends much less time on the couch and hopes to persuade others to do the same.

Made in the USA
Charleston, SC
07 December 2016